Evaluation and Accountability in Human Service Programs

Edited by William C. Sze
June G. Hopps

SCHENKMAN PUBLISHING COMPANY, INC.
Cambridge, Massachusetts

TABLE OF CONTENTS

FOREWORD

The evaluation of human service programs has suddenly emerged as one of the most pervasive and pressing concerns of the helping professions. A subject which formerly attracted the interest of only a few persons currently commands the attention of an increasing number of practitioners, researchers and scholars in various disciplines.

In this timely publication, which contains a comprehensive bibliography, the authors examine the social, political and organizational context of evaluation research; discuss alternative models for program evaluation and experimental design; describe three projects from different fields of service; and provide a critical overview of the current state of program evaluation.

This book is the product of a Symposium on this subject sponsored by The Ohio State University School of Social Work held on the campus at the Fawcett Center for Tomorrow, June 10-12, 1973. The idea for the Symposium originated with the Faculty Research Committee of the School of Social Work. Initially, the Committee intended to plan an activity for the purpose of enabling the faculty of the School to increase their knowledge and develop their skill in this area. As discussion and planning proceeded, the Committee became acutely aware of the magnitude of concern about the evaluation of human service programs. Consequently, plans were expanded to conduct a Symposium that would enable persons other than faculty to participate and to publish a document which would be a major contribution to the literature in this field.

Professors June Hopps and William Sze, in addition to serving as co-editors of this volume, carried major responsibilities for conceptualizing, developing and coordinating the details of the Symposium. James R. McCoy, Dean of the College, and Associate Dean and Director of the Research Division, Dr. Reed M. Powell, provided extremely helpful expertise, resources, and encouragement for the project. Jamie Smith e' Incas, M.D., Director of Human Resources, Columbus Model City Program, and Harry E. Allen, Ph.D., Director of the Program for the Study of Crime and Delinquency at The Ohio State University, participated in the Symposium discussion sessions. Their papers were not available for publication. Ms. Amy Arrington provided the excellent typing skills that were necessary in this effort.

To the editors and contributors of this volume, I extend my grateful appreciation. It is the hope of everyone who contributed to this volume that its readers will be inspired to undertake better research to discover new insights about the evaluation of human service programs.

Richard R. Medhurst, Director
School of Social Work
College of Administrative Science
The Ohio State University
Columbus, Ohio
November 16, 1973

LIST OF CONTRIBUTORS

Behling, John H., Ph.D., Associate Professor of Social Work at The Ohio State University.

Coke, James G., Ph.D., Professor of Political Science, Kent State University and Director, Public Policy Analysis Office, Office of the Governor, State of Ohio.

D'Angelo, Rocco D., Ph.D., Associate Professor of Social Work and Director, Teenage Flight Research Project at The Ohio State University.

Duncan, Joseph W., Ph.D., Corporate Coordinator of Urban Affairs, Battelle Memorial Institute, Columbus, Ohio.

Eaton, Joseph W., Ph.D., Professor of Sociology and Social Work at the University of Pittsburgh.

Franklin, Clyde W. Jr., Ph.D., Associate Professor of Sociology at the Ohio State University.

Hansan, John E., M.S.W., Chief of Staff, Office of the Governor, State of Ohio.

Higgs, Louis D., Ph.L., Program Specialist, the Public Sector Office of the National Science Foundation, Washington, D.C.

Hoffer, Joe R., Ph.D., Visiting Professor of Social Work at The Ohio State University and Former Executive Secretary, National Conference on Social Welfare.

Hopps, June G., Ph.D., Associate Professor of Social Work and Chairperson, Research Sequence at The Ohio State University. Commissioner of Rehabilitation Services, State of Ohio.

Nagi, Saad Z., Ph.D., Professor of Sociology and Physical Medicine, Mershon Research Center at The Ohio State University and Project Director, National Study on Child Abuse.

Parnes, Herbert S., Ph.D., Professor of Economics and Director of Human Resources Research Center at The Ohio State University.

Parnicky, Joseph J., Ph.D., Professor of Social Work and Director of Social Service of Nisonger Center at The Ohio State University.

Schneiderman, Leonard, Ph.D., Professor of Social Work and Director of Ohio Public Assistance and Vocational Rehabilitation Expansion Grants Evaluation Project at The Ohio State University.

Sze, William C., Ph.D., Associate Professor of Social Work at
The Ohio State University.
Turner, John B., D.S.W., Dean and Professor of the School of
Applied Social Sciences, Case Western Reserve Univer-
sity.
Warren, Roland L., Ph.D., Professor of Community Theory,
Florence Heller Graduate School for Advanced Studies in
Social Welfare at Brandeis University.
Washington, Robert, Ph.D., Assistant Professor and Chief
Researcher, East Cleveland Project at Case Western
Reserve University.
Weiss, Carol H., Ph.D., Senior Research Associate, Bureau of
Applied Social Research at Columbia University.

INTRODUCTION

A Preview

Social problems have plagued civilization from time immemorial. Determined attempts to deal with these problems have been launched repeatedly, particularly during the second half of the twentieth century. Much painful experience has been acquired from each new attempt but such experience has rarely been in a form readily available and useful to those initiating new programs.

Part of the difficulty has arisen because human service programming has not traditionally been concerned with the effectiveness of its performance. In the past it was assumed that any program with the stated purpose of helping people and solving human problems necessarily had great social value and therefore should be supported without question. This assumption is no longer accepted. Social programming now exists within a societal framework highly influenced by technological development and the old assumptions and tacit beliefs come under the scrutiny of an educated, scientifically sophisticated citizenry. As a result, human services are entering a new era—the age of accountability.

To meet new standards of accountability demanded by this changing concept of public and community services, social scientists have been developing various models and methods. The age of accountability is characterized by attempts to put program planning, development and evaluation into a circular form with rational, analytical and objective components that will provide logical growth of programs, making use of past experience in a way that leads to increased productivity. A good example of this kind of approach is the Planning, Programming and Budgeting System (PPBS) which has exerted a great impact on the Federal government. This system was first developed by the Defense Department for weapon systems development and control, and it has been used extensively by the Department of Health, Education and Welfare for planning and evaluation.

Any attempt to provide accountability in human services results in a recognition of the need for formal criteria for the most basic considerations of program planning. Rivlin suggested that one in the position of decision-making relative to social action programs would want answers to the following questions:

1. How do we define the problems, and how are they distributed? Who is poor or sick or inadequately educated?
2. Who would be helped by specific social action programs, and how much?
3. What would do the most good? How do the benefits of different kinds of programs compare?
4. How can particular kinds of social services be produced most effectively?[1]

In examining this series of complex questions, one can appreciate the fact that only through systematic evaluation research can meaningful answers be formulated.

We will attempt to point out several major areas of concern in evaluation research which unfortunately have not been given serious attention by those researchers who are preoccupied with the importance of quantitative methodology and theory building and therefore have overlooked some vital issues. The issues we allude to are related primarily to the area of institutional and human predicaments. If the following predicaments are not given sufficient consideration, we feel many research findings become tenuous. The predicaments here to be considered are: (1) The difficulty in defining social problems and hence goals of social programs; (2) The difficulty in maintaining objectivity; (3) The difficulty in avoiding contamination by social and human constraints; and (4) Organizational and institutional forces exerted on the researcher.

The difficulty in defining social problems and hence goals of social programs. Who defines a social problem—a lay person or a social scientist? The fact is that everyone has his own viewpoint on a social problem and often assumes he knows the answer to the problem. Even when social scientists get together to analyze and define a social problem, there are great variations in viewpoint. Since most social problems are extremely complex in nature, with intertwining multiple causes, the attempt to define the problem and its solution boils down to the question of determining the relative importance of those multiple causes. The same kind of dilemma is encountered in defining program goals. The following statement from a report to Congress on evaluation of the performance of the Job Corps illustrates the difficulty in defining the goals of a human service program.

> Past experience indicates that more than 40 percent of all enrollees drop out or are discharged from the program within three months of enrollment. It could be argued that for those who stay such a short time, the Job Corps experience constitutes another failure with little, if any, positive impact upon the life of dropouts. Spokesmen for the Job Corps, however, insist that even a short stay in the Job Corps is not a total loss since the enrollees receive counseling, medical treatment, and are fed and housed. Job Corps officials also maintain that average annual costs exaggerate the true investment per enrollee because most corpsmen complete their course of study in less than a year. This claim that the prescribed curriculum can be mastered by deficiently educated youth in less than a year, however, raises questions about the quality and quantity of education and training offered at the centers. [2]

Is the goal of the Job Corps to provide a job, (i.e., any job) or is it developing clients to their fullest potential? Is the goal to provide counseling, and medical care, even though the recipients do not stay with the program long enough to get a job? Is its goal to provide a bare minimum of education that a disadvantaged youth can absorb in a given time span, or is it to provide education bringing the youth to a given level of accomplishment? If all these possible goals are desirable, how shall they be ranked as to priority, and to determine justification of monies spent? Goal definition becomes an extremely complex task indeed. Other human services may differ in subject content, but not in difficulty when specificity is sought in determining goals. Despite Suchman's suggestion that the definition of the objective of a human service program is to be considered as one of the primary steps leading to meaningful evaluative research,[3] as Rivlin pointed out, "most social action programs have vague and diverse goals and agreement on how to measure their success is far from complete."[4]

The difficulty in maintaining objectivity. Subjective feelings and individual bias creep in when the program administrator, or even occasionally the evaluator, justify their claims on the basis of their belief in the high humanistic purpose of the program rather than solely on the outcome of the service as originally proposed. The comment frequently goes like this: Although the program fell short of expectations, it was still worth the expense; or at least it is better than spending the taxpayer's money on the Viet-Nam War. Another type of subjective justification can be called the "Serendipity Bonanza." Referring back to the Job Corps report as an example, the spokesman for the Corps contended that even if they failed to achieve their principal objective, the residual benefit experienced as an unanticipated by-product of the program was by itself significant enough to justify preserving the program. If this type of argument prevails, every program would find a raison d'etre. As a result, the usefulness of, or the faith in the program evaluation will be diminished significantly.

The difficulty in avoiding contamination by social and human constraints. The uncertainty of interpretation of findings is in part due to the complexity of social causation which social scientists find difficult to pinpoint. For instance, how many factors should be considered in order to evaluate the effectiveness of any given program? A given factor may not appear to be essential initially, but may still turn out to be a key factor for the success or failure of a program, with a resulting dilemma in evaluation. To return to the Job Corps example again, we see this dilemma clearly. The final objective of the Job Corps is to train school dropouts to obtain gainful employment upon the completion of the Corps' program. Question arises over the extent to which evaluation should account for other social and human factors such as the current job market, trade union membership restraints, unfair civil rights practices in that community, the trainee's personality composition, etc. No doubt these factors can significantly affect the statistical findings of the gainful employment rate of those Job Corps graduates. If the finding shows that only 25% of the trainees are employed after the program, can we conclude that the low rate of gainful employment is a reflection of the ineffective program, or an artifact of current unemployment rates, job discrimination practices, etc. Another constraint to effective evaluation is the temporal aspect of effects. Most community action programs are sponsored by an administration which has strong political investment to the success or failure of its regime which will have a relatively short life span unless growth and development of its programs are immediately apparent. This creates a sense of urgency on the time dimension, yet it should be realized that in dealing with human service, individual differences must be considered.[5] Some individuals experience a "delayed reaction," giving the program efforts what Hyman and Wright[6] call the "sleeper effect." They suggest that "if a program aims at affecting the conduct of its audience, a long-range time perspective may be vital, since certain kinds of behavior may require a relatively long time span before the individuals involved have an opportunity to behave as expected."[7] The predicament for the program evaluator lies in reconciling the sponsoring agency's demands for a fast result on the one hand, and the need for longer observation to avoid spurious effects on the other.

Organizational and institutional forces exerted on the researcher. The odds are against a truly revealing report which might damage the image of the agency. As Mann cogently observed: "Most evaluative investigations are instituted to 'prove' something in which people already believe. The researcher is generally aware of how the study is supposed to turn out. If the conclusions are not as expected, the researcher may be penalized if he or she is unfortunate enough to depend on the institution for full-time employment beyond the duration of the project. In this context, research is viewed more as a method of social validation than as an impersonal guide to the truth."[8] In the same vein, Rossi added this observation: "When a research finding shows that a program is ineffective, and the research director has failed to plan for this eventuality, then the impact can be so devastating that it becomes more comforting to deny the worth of the negative evaluation than to reorganize one's planning."[9] As Campbell rightly pointed out, the administrator confronted with a complex situation which is the product of custom, politics, human foibles plus monetary and other realistic limitations views evaluation and projected reform with a callous eye. Reforms are characteristically offered as though they were certain of success, and most frequently stem from sources with great possible political impact on the program. The genuine difficulties in implementing reforms may be blithely ignored. The administrator facing this combination of factors, and experienced in the slow, painful pace of institutional change may see his wisest course of action as the limiting of evaluation to areas he can most directly control, particularly if the evaluation is to be published or otherwise made public. The consequences of this outlook and practice have devastating effects on the hopes for significant evaluation, and must receive primary consideration if credibility and the ethics of proper utilization of the evaluative findings are to be preserved.[10] In view of the above discussion and comments we have to be aware of the consequences of such practices in order to preserve the credibility and ethics of the utilization of evaluative findings.

Hence, all in all, the issues we have mentioned so far have certainly contributed to the retardation of the proper development of this vital research field and its value and means for solving social and human problems.

Organization of this volume

Materials presented here are organized into four topical parts: Macroscopic Problems, Technological Problems, Profiles in Evaluation Research, and Commentary and Bibliography.

Macroscopic Problems are those that relate to the larger contexts in which evaluation and accountability studies are conceived, planned and implemented. In Part I, consideration is given to the impact of social, political and organizational behavior whose effects lie outside the traditional or microscopic level of research controls or manipulation such as experimental design, measurement and quantification. As Warren suggested, the researcher who is concerned with the validity of evaluation research performed at the microscopic level should be equally concerned with the transferability of these microscopically valid findings within a proper perspective; namely some general macroscopic framework or social context. To adequately address these issues concerned with the macroscopic character of evaluation research implies, of course, the existence of widely acceptable macroscopic formulations or models which can provide a comprehensive framework within which evaluation research can be efficiently performed. Such comprehensive models, though surely needed, are virtually non-existent and their development should constitute one of the high priority long-range objectives of the social scientist.

This admittedly is an awesome task, beset with many obstacles, not the least of which are conflicting interests, ideologies and a knowledge of how to evaluate various goals in quantitative ways. The social and psychological consequences of intervention are difficult even to contemplate, let alone predict. Thus the concept of evaluation research could well be expanded so that it also provides experiemental testing of elements of macroscopic considerations and together with other inputs provide the basic quantitative parameters required in the scientific shaping of a suitable integrated microscopic framework. The need for such a framework and some of the ingredients thereof is highlighted in Roland Warren's paper on "The Social Context of Program Evaluation Research."

When individuals, corporations and public agencies consider embarking upon or opposing a particular economic or business endeavor, they attempt to project the gains and losses to themselves and the decision they make usually is based upon what they believe will maximize their gains and minimize their losses. Decisions for social intervention, however, are many times more complex, arising out of a multiplicity of decisions in public and private sectors. When these bodies consider an intervention program they attempt to project the potential gains and losses to the target population, to themselves, and/or to various non-target constituencies. One generally finds that decisions in these instances are attempts to optimize results with respect to a multiplicity of population segments, the relative weighting in the optimization process depending upon the particular intervention program and the public or private organization principally involved in the decision-making.

Almost without exception, however, social intervention will affect some people or interests beneficially and others adversely. There is yet no accepted arithmetic or formula which one may employ to clearly subtract the pains from the pleasures in order to determine a measure of social desirability. How are the interests of suburban commuters and the residents of the inner-city to be balanced in the evaluation of transportation intervention strategies? Uncertainties about the effects abound and in the final analysis most decisions may be viewed as determinations of where the burden of uncertainty should fall. Thus unlike intervention in technology and the economic marketplace we find that the goals of social intervention strategies, either by design or the lack thereof, often lack clarity or completeness of specification. The problem has aspects that are intrinsically of a political and/or bureaucratic nature.

Two papers, in addition to Warren's, and the commentary thereupon complete Part I of this volume. The paper by Coke and Hansan is an enlightening and cutting treatment of the political context of evaluation research and the pragmatic environment in which it is performed. The principal problems dealt with by Nagi in his discussion of gate-keeping decisions are bureaucratic in nature, showing explicitly how structure and decisions within bureaucracies can affect, and in fact sometimes completely negate, the usefulness of evaluation research findings. All of the contributors in this section raise fundamental questions regarding the effects of the traditional research approach on the reliability and validity of program evaluation.

In Part II of this volume the contributors deal with some of the methodological problems of evaluation research. Weiss considers several of the fixed design models for evaluation research including the more recent accountability system model. In contrast Higgs deals principally with the newly emerging dynamic research design models which are applications of the more general applied mathematical methods of dynamic programming to problems of social policy decision making. Higgs refers to his model of experimental design in evaluation research as a "Multistage Decision Process."

Several papers related to case material are presented in Part III. These papers, based on the practical experiences of the researchers, deal with problems encountered in program intervention, ranging from individual functioning to community related issues, and provide insights to many of the ideas presented in the preceding discussion. Washington and Turner consider issues that are encountered when evaluating an integrated service program in an urban satellite community that has recently undergone residential change. The paper was based on experiences at the East Cleveland Project where systems theory and a behavioral approach to service delivery are frameworks for evaluation. The paper by Parnicky focuses on evaluation issues in the field of mental retardation. Several evaluation research models and their utility to mental retardation are reviewed. Parnicky notes that a new human service program evaluation model is emerging which draws heavily from the concepts of mental retardation, deviance and normalization and predicts that it is likely to expand research efforts in the application of the normalization principle to retarded individuals. Problems in community focused research with teenage runaways is dealt with by D'Angelo. The difficulties the evaluation researcher encounters when attempting to consciously encourage members of a community to participate in a research area that is sensitive to them are dilineated. The hindsights and insights of these researchers should prove helpful to the reader.

In the final part of the volume a critique and a commentary of the papers presented in Parts I and II is given by Schneiderman and a bibliographical chapter is provided by Hopps and Sze. Schneiderman's summary is provocatively critical, taking issue with certain aspects of each of the papers. As important as the critical features is the degree to which he has met the challenge of gleaning from the diverse positions presented in this volume concerning the various ideological and methodological issues associated with the surmounting problem of evaluation research. Hopps and Sze provide an extensive bibliography and discussion on the developmental perspective of program evaluation. Four areas of human service references are presented; namely, Social Service, Social Action Programs, Mental Health and Health Care. Additionally, a list of readings in the general area of program evaluation are also included.

In conclusion, this book has illustrated the complex nature and crucial issues in program evaluation. There have been some philosophical and methodological differences among the contributors and commentators. As a result, a variety of views are represented in this volume. This will give students of evaluative research an opportunity to get acquainted with some of the major issues and predicaments which face every program evaluator. Furthermore, we hope that this book will stimulate readers to examine their own position regarding program evaluation and subsequently further aimed at the improvement and development of their evaluation strategy within their own particular research environment.

Footnotes for Introduction

[1] Alice M. Rivlin, *Systematic Thinking for Social Action*, The Brookings Institution, Washington, D. C., 1971, pp. 6-7.

[2] *Examination of the War on Poverty, Staff and Consultants Reports*, prepared for the Subcommittee on Employment, Manpower, and Poverty of the Committee on Labor and Public Welfare, United States Senate on Job Corps Neighborhood Youth Corps Work Experience Role of Private Enterprise, Vol. 1, August, 1967, p. 11.

[3] Edward A. Suchman, *Evaluative Research*, Russell Sage Foundation, New York, 1967, p. 7.

[4] Alice M. Rivlin, *Systematic Thinking for Social Action*, The Brookings Institution, Washington, D. C., 1971, p. 127.

[5] Michael P. Brooks, "The Community Action Program as a Setting for Applied Research," *Journal of Social Issues*, Vol. 21, 1965, pp. 39-40.

[6] Herbert H. Hyman and Charles R. Wright, "Evaluating Social Action Programs," in Francis G. Caro (ed.), *Readings in Evaluation Research*, Russell Sage Foundation, New York, 1971, p. 200.

[7] *Ibid,*. p. 200.

[8] John Mann, "Technical and Social Difficulties in the Conduct of Evaluative Research," in *Changing Human Behavior*, Charles Scribner's Sons, Inc., 1965, pp. 188-189.

[9] Peter H. Rossi, "Evaluating Social Actions Programs," in Francis G. Caro, (ed.), *Readings in Evaluation Research*, Russell Sage Foundation, New York, 1971, p. 278.

[10] Donald T. Campbell, "Reforms as Experiments," in Francis G. Caro (ed.), *Readings in Evaluation Research*, Russell Sage Foundation, New York, 1971, pp. 233-234.

PART I

THE MACROSCOPIC PROBLEMS

CHAPTER 1

The Social Context of
Program Evaluation Research

Ronald L. Warren

Part of the growing interest and excitement surrounding program evaluation research is the paradox of its great promise for more effective intervention techniques into the major problems of society in the future and its extremely modest performance in affecting those intervention techniques in the present. A review of the burgeoning literature on social program evaluation research suggests two major problem areas of enduring concern. The bulk of concern centers around the problem of adequate methodology on the one hand and the problem of what may be called the social context of evaluation research on the other. It is supposedly in these areas that progress must be made if evaluation research is to have its full potential impact on the organized ways in which American society confronts its social problems.

The first area of concern is the extent to which evaluation research methodologies actually result in definitive findings in response to the questions which they address. To oversimplify, the problem can be summed up in the question: Do the studies actually validly indicate the nature and extent of impact which a particular program or project has had on a specified group of people? I do not intend to pursue in this paper the ramified methodological questions which are implicit in this major question. Suffice it to say that unless we can be confident of the validity of the findings of such studies, we can hardly be surprised at skepticism on the part of agencies whose programs the findings often challenge, and we can hardly be satisfied that we are adding to the storehouse of scientific knowledge.

The second problem is equally complex. It deals with the conditions which are necessary if valid evaluation research is to be successfully conducted and if its findings are to be given optimum utilization in modifying or replacing agency programs. In some cases, conditions in the social environment make it impossible to preserve the integrity of the research design, so that plans which were put together with great elegance and virtuosity suffer attrition or destruction in the course of the research process.

It would be difficult to overemphasize the importance of these two companion problems of methodological soundness and of agency reception and implementation. They both must be resolved with increasing competence if evaluation research is to fulfill its promising potential. Anyone who is familiar with the excellent books on evaluation research by Suchman, Caro, and Weiss can attest to the serious attention being given by scholars to various aspects of these two important problems. What one does not find in them or in other analogous publications is a broad consideration of the larger social context in which evaluation researchers define their problem, establish their methodology, produce their findings, and make their recommendations. In this paper, I will attempt such an analysis.

The Fragmentary Intervention Program and the Controlled Field Experiment: A Convergence

Let us begin by noting a peculiar convergence of scientific research traditions with the structuring of social agencies and social programs addressed to various social problems. I refer on the one hand to the scientific tradition of the controlled experiment, and on the other to the structuring of agency intervention techniques into specific, limited intervention strategies. Great demonstrable progress, most notably in the natural sciences, has been made by the procedure of holding everything constant in two situations except the one variable whose effect is to be measured. Differences shown in two groups or situations on a before and after basis, with only the single variable being changed, can be attributed to the change in that experimental variable. Although the description is here highly oversimplified, especially in reference to the employment of intermediate variables and of various control variables in differing experimental situations, the basic methodology of the controlled experiment is captured in the simple injunction: Hold all else constant, manipulate only one variable at a time, and measure the results. We all are aware of the many difficulties of trying to accomplish this, methodologically, in social research. Such difficulties are widely addressed in the evaluation research literature. Because of them, it is often not possible to apply rigorously the full methodology of the controlled field experiment. Yet it is widely recognized as the most desirable methodology for impact evaluation purposes. In this paper, the term will also be used to include methodologies which approach but do not reach all of the requirements of the controlled field experiment.

The basic methodology of the controlled field experiment is peculiarly adaptable to the actual situation regarding agency programs. For the basic mode of operation of individual agencies which intervene in the lives of various target populations is to seek some presumably critical point of leverage and to intervene at that point. Most programs do not address the total living situation of the target population, but for various reasons of practice and practicality they confine themselves to a very limited, relatively identifiable type of intervention, while all other things in the life situation of the target population are "held constant" in that they are left unaltered.

How natural, then, for social scientists to come along and in effect say: Look, we have a research method for dealing with such situations as this. You are intervening in a total living configuration, and your intervention can be considered as a single variable which is being changed. We have the ideal method to test it: The controlled field experiment.

One might summarize this situation by saying that through evaluation research, social scientists can aid agency effectiveness by doing what they know how to do best in relation to agency professionals who in turn are doing what they know how to do best—a happy convergence. Among the benefactors are the target populations, who presumably now have some assurance that programs which do not help them will be weeded out, and that from the accumulated knowledge gained through such evaluations, more effective programs will not only be developed but will be tested rigorously for their demonstrable benign impact.

But even more important, a way has been found to put science in the service of beneficence, to continuously hone and improve programs addressed to human betterment. As my colleague Howard Freeman somewhat enthusiastically writes, citing Campbell: "We may not be there yet, but we are moving in the direction of becoming an experimental society."[1]

True, problems of methodology and of the proper reception and adequate implementation of evaluation research findings still abound, but they are being dealt with, incrementally, as experience and knowledge accumulate in this promising new field.

Yet every rose has thorns. One of the principal difficulties is that so many evaluation studies turn out to have negative findings. This has two disquieting consequences. The first has been recognized for a long time. The reports get buried; or they are attacked on the basis of their methodology. In Rossi's words:

> Methodological unsophisticates suddenly become experts in sampling, questionnaire construction, experimental design, and statistical analysis, or borrow experts for the occasion. Apparently, you can always find some expert who will be able to find something wrong with the research.[2]

And what is worse, he reminds us that: "It is difficult to recall any social-action program that was put out of business by a negative evaluation."

But the difficulties go beyond individual agencies resisting admonishments. The problems which the agencies are addressing through fragmented intervention strategies must be questioned if the evaluation researchers are to test effectively.

Although the atomized fragmented one-variable-at-a-time approach is typically assumed to be the appropriate mode of evaluation studies, Carol Weiss has pointed out that its results to date should indicate the need for a drastic change in terms of social policy:

> In the deepest sense, there is nothing null about recent evaluation research. The newly-visible large-scale evaluations are progressively disclosing the bankruptcy of piecemeal approaches to social programming. Unless society's limited domestic resources are invested more wisely, significant changes are not likely to occur. This is as important a conclusion as evaluation can provide.[3]

In this important passage, Carol Weiss used the word "evaluation" rather than "evaluation research." In my estimation, this was both appropriate and instructive. For the evaluation research itself does not suggest the bankruptcy of piecemeal approaches. Rather, it is the accumulation of research findings on many programs, as these are in turn examined, assessed, and evaluated in a process of rational analysis which itself however, is not evaluation research, not experimental design, but rather rational, informed analysis—

trying to make sense out of facts. What it suggests is the need for a more inclusive process of informed, rational assessment, which is not experimental design and cannot be reduced to experimental design. It is rather a process of trying to put together what we know—from social theory, from practice experience, and from evaluation research efforts, in order to assess the general configuration. In doing so, we must go beyond individual research projects, the improvement of research design, and the gaining of competence in administering research projects and presenting findings in ways conducive to their acceptance and utilization. We also need to think—always a difficult assignment.

Let me state the situation a different way. Evaluation researchers frequently criticize agencies for ignoring the findings of evaluation research and going right on administering programs which research proves ineffective. Now, in aggregating all these negative research results from individual projects, we presume to extract an important admonition for society: Give up the useless myopia of fragmented programs which address only one small part of the social context. Rather, start to do something about the total living configuration of target populations, including the institutional configuration within which they develop their problems and become target populations.

But if there is a lesson here for society and for the agencies, is there not an analogous lesson for evaluation researchers? Putting this another way, if on the basis of the research findings we are asking the agencies to stop doing what they best know how to do and to start taking a more inclusive view? Should we not ask the same thing of evaluation researchers? Or, once they acknowledge the essential inadequacy of piecemeal intervention approaches, will they continue to expend their major efforts in continued evaluation of yet additional piecemeal approaches, with only an occasional admonition that both parties—the agencies and the evaluators—are on the wrong track? Will they continue—like the agencies—to do what they best know how to do and ignore the implications of their own previous findings?

I say "what they best know how to do," because what evaluation researchers best know how to do is to study intensively the impact of piecemeal programs. The more piecemeal, the fewer the experimental variables involved, the more applicable is the research design. By contrast, there is no known methodology—other than informed rational analysis—for definitive findings regarding the functioning of larger systems. There are technologies at this level, but they have not yet proved adequate to the task, and I believe that it is because of their inherent limitations rather than remediable defects in the present state of technology. Examples are costs-benefits analysis and systems analysis. Neither of them contributes, or is designed to contribute, to substantive theoretical understanding of the interrelationship of different parts of the institutional context, including different agency policies and programs, as they affect the lives of people and contribute, in aggregate, to a remarkably steady state of identifiable production of various pathologies.

Guba has put it well:

> Thus, the introduction of various *levels* of evaluation introduces problems that are by no means able to be resolved through the application of techniques, methods, criteria and perspectives developed at the micro level, where we are accustomed to working.... Evaluators must learn to "think big," and thinking big involves more than a quantitative increase in perspective.[4]

Adequacies and Inadequacies of Conventional Evaluation Research

My principal thesis is that conventional evaluation research fragmentalizes the problems which the intervention is supposed to address in such a way that the problems are largely insoluble at that level and hence the findings, whether positive or negative, are often largely irrelevant to the problems addressed. By accepting the fragmented agency intervention strategy as a point of departure, the evaluation research naively accepts the agency's implicit definition of the causes of the problem and of the nature of the proposed remedies for it. He thus jumps into the intervention evaluation process without having given systematic attention to the question of diagnosis. In doing so, he abdicates his role as a social scientist, and renounces his potentially most important contribution: To investigate critically the nature of problem definition, the social dynamics of the phenomena which are defined as social problems, their interrelation with other parts of social structures and social processes, and the development of proposed programs of intervention on such broad bases. This is his principal contribution as a social scientist, not the technically elegant conducting of evaluation research on problems defined by others and intervention techniques which he knows are fragmentary and which have often been devised precisely without the kind of depth diagnosis of the problems which he as a social scientist is presumably competent to offer. Then, reviewing the situation that many evaluation studies are negative in their findings, he suggests the need—presumably for other people—to do what he as a social scientist has voluntarily renounced—patient analytical investigation of the total social context surrounding the "problem" behavior.

My point in asserting and elaborating on this thesis is not to condemn evaluation research, but to urge its broadening out from the myopia induced by the convergence of experimental design and piecemealed agency intervention techniques. In pursuing this point, let us examine the preconditions for the relevant and effective application of controlled field experiments to intervention programs. Quite aside from the stringent methodological preconditions and constraints of this evaluational approach, I am turning attention to the question of the requisites for the logical justification of its application to specific intervention situations.

The procedure becomes more and more relevant and logically justifiable to the extent that:

1. In the condition's causal pattern, a single identifiable element accounts for most of the variance;

2. A specific intervention strategy is available which with good reason is believed:

a. to be controllable by the agency through its intervention program,

b. to have massive impact in itself, or in combination with other variables which are known and are similarly under the control of the agency and will be simultaneously applied.

There are additional considerations, which bear more directly on the specific methodology but which are often ignored. An example is the question of the extent to which the meanings used in the evaluation are sufficient and valid measures of the condition whose remedy is being sought through the intervention. Putting this another way, even if positive findings ensue, in many cases the measures employed are such that positive findings are virtually inconsequential, in that they do not address the major dimensions of the problem.

But this question relates to methodological rigor, which though important is not my present topic. I mention it only because questions of this type are often overlooked in a mere preoccupation with technical procedures of research. Since validity is one of the most difficult things to measure quantitatively, it tends to receive only superficial attention, while primary attention continues to be placed on greater quantitative precision.

Returning to the preconditions for the field experiment model, I would suggest that they are seldom adequately met, and that to the extent that they are not met the research problem definition is inadequate, the intervention strategy is of only minor consequence, and the methodology of investigation is largely misplaced.

Do we really take seriously what has been learned in the social sciences about multiple causation? What it indicates is that in most problem situations there is no single element which either causes the problem condition or can be used to correct or measurably ameliorate the problem condition. In many problem areas, informed rational analysis is sufficient to cast grave doubt on single intervention techniques designed to make significant impacts on admittedly complex situations.

Let me present an outstanding example of what I consider to be the essential naivete' and myopia which I have described. A number of years ago a rather extensive demonstration project was developed, directed at so-called multi-problem families. The intervention technique was that of intensive casework with considerable inter-agency cooperation and many of the other desiderata which at the time were considered to be at the cutting edge of new developments in family casework. A careful evaluation research design was developed, which contained not only a utilization of the classical controlled field experiment model, but many of the other appurtenances of sophisticated field research methodology. It was, in its design, "one for the books," and has been frequently cited in the evaluation research literature. The principal investigator in the research later wrote that both researchers and caseworkers were well aware that no effectiveness might be shown by the demonstration program. I quote:

> We even joked about it in a sort of macabre fashion, but I don't think any of us really anticipated such an outcome. Nevertheless, we all had our own little ways of hedging. Mine was to say,

"If the demonstration proves effective, we will have to rewrite all the books." To my way of thinking, intensive casework services could offer, even under the best circumstances, such a small part of the total configuration of attitudes, behavior patterns, and institutional configurations surrounding these troubled families that it would seem miraculous if casework could have a sufficient effect to be registered on the admittedly crude instruments we planned to use. The instruments were the best available.[5]

But this notion that "if the demonstration proves effective, we will have to rewrite all the books" did not deter the evaluation researcher from proceeding. The project and the evaluation research were carried through as planned. No significant differences on the outcome measures were found between the experimental group of target families and the control group.

If it appears that I am pointing a self-righteous, holier-than-thou finger at this researcher, let me be the first to assert what many of you already know: that I was that evaluation researcher. And so quite obviously, to the extent that my remarks are critical they certainly apply to me.

Peter Rossi has asserted that the principal reason so much evaluation research produces negative findings is that, in a sense, the major social measures we know about have already been applied. What is left is the possibility of only marginal improvements at high cost. He writes:

A supplementary preschool program attempting to bring poor and otherwise disadvantaged children into parity with those better off because of family background would appear to be an excellent program. But any such program is not likely to produce as much benefit as did the introduction of elementary schooling.[6]

Thus, the cream has been skimmed off the top of social reform efforts, so that each successive measure tends to show diminishing results. This major mode of accounting for the largely negative or inconsequential results of many evaluation projects carries a great deal of credibility, at least with me. But let us pursue it further. What it states is that from incremental measures, largely inconsequential results may be expected. It does not state that as a matter of fact, all the major innovation methods—which would correspond roughly to universal free education—have already been applied. And indeed they have not. As a single example, many manpower training programs have been found to have little effectiveness. But in this field, there are major measures which might be taken, corresponding to universal free education, which have not been taken. An analogue in the employment field might therefore be universal provision of employment opportuniies at wages above the poverty level. So in many manpower training programs, and in other areas as well, we are applying only incremental efforts in areas where major efforts have not yet been made, efforts which would be the counterpart of universal free education or, in the health field, of modern sanitation practices or the provision of potable water. This is a matter of evaluation, is it not, even though it seems rather remote from evaluation research? Can we not bring the two closer together?

It would appear that social scientists engaged in evaluation research might perform a service by using their special competence as social scientists in what I have called informed rational analysis. To do this they must be willing to deal with what is not readily measurable, and they must open themselves up to accusations of "subjectivity." And to do it, they must be less bound by the constraints of accepting the funding agency's definition of the problem than they now are.

Such considerations are, I believe, not unrelated to the purportedly low esteem in which evaluation research is held by many social scientists. It is looked down upon as sort of "second-rate" social science, an almost exclusively technical occupation rather than a scientific one, which does not advance theoretical understanding but rather provides a means of helping administrators solve their practical problems—sort of an adjunct of operations research.

Such criticisms are in part ill-founded. But is it not possible that part of the reason for the low esteem of evaluation researchers is both well-taken and remediable: Namely, that in many instances they really do abdicate their role as social scientists with substantive knowledge as well as technical competence in research? That they do not concern themselves with a substantive assessment of the intervention technique, but only with the rigorous methodology for testing its effects? That they all-too-willingly accept agency- defined problems and agency-defined intervention techniques? That often what they do is actually therefore inconsequential from the standpoint of social science? To the extent that this is the case, it need not be. Later I shall offer some specific suggestions as to how it might be altered.

In connection with the relatively low position of evaluation researchers vis-a-vis their funding agencies, Carol Weiss has written:

> The new-style evaluation money, although larger in amount than ever before, comes ringed around with restrictions. Not only do the government "RFPs" (request for proposal, the specifications of the research to be done and its scheduling) specify many of the details of objectives, indicators, timing, analysis, and reporting which used to be thought of as the evaluator's bailiwick, but government agencies are requiring increasingly close surveillance during the course of the study. Some are requiring biweekly conferences or monthly reports. The reason is, clearly, the sad experience that many agencies have had with evaluation. Academic evaluators have been known to bend the purposes of the study to suit their own disciplinary interests.[7]

She goes on to give glaring examples of such distortion on the part of academic evaluators. But clearly, the choice need not be between the social scientist abdicating his scientific role to do a purely technical job for the agency, or the social scientist exploiting the research money for his own irrelevant academic interests. There is a wide range between these extremes for the social scientist to utilize what leeway he is given, and to continue to press for more—not to depart from the subject matter of the evaluation, but to subject it to an evaluation which is in keeping with his special knowledge and analytical ability as a social scientist. If he has no special knowledge or analytical ability as a social scientist which can be brought to bear on the program being evaluated, then of course we must concede that his capacity is purely technical and he would perhaps be well advised to remain within that technical capacity. Whether or not social scientists who do have such capacity really should or would confine their engagement with a problem purely to the technical aspects of conventional research evaluation constitutes the question I am addressing. If they are willing to assume solely the role of a technician, they or we should not be surprised that they become so regarded by their academic colleagues.

Latent Effects of Conventional Evaluation Research

It is perhaps banal to remind ourselves that social scientists are part of the subject matter they are investigating and that their research behavior and findings feed back into the social process they are studying. We all know this. Yet we often ignore its implications; or once acknowledging them, we brush them aside to get on with our business. What is fed back into the social process is sometimes not so much the specific findings which we mean to communicate, as rather the latent functions which our conceptual formulations and our research activities perform. This is particularly important in the case of evaluation research.

Let us consider the convergence of controlled field experimental methods and the agencies' need to test specific, often fragmented intervention programs. By limiting our attention to the presumed impact of a single highly fragmentalized input variable and by ignoring the importance of all other variables by means of control groups and randomization, the inadvertent assumption is communicated that all other aspects of the configuration are to be taken as fixed, or given. They are parts of social reality to which we adjust. The appropriate manner to intervene is at the level and with the substance of the intervention technique under scrutiny.

Again, program evaluation research is usually directed at specific target populations, usually "problem" populations of some type. The intervention is an attempt to change *them.* Quite obviously, this carries with it the implicit assumption that they constitute the problem; the problem would not exist were it not for them; if they changed in certain desired ways there would no longer be a problem. Merely to make this implicit assumption explicit is to reveal its speciousness. Yet the latent effect of much evaluation research is to reinforce such a conceptualization of the problem, to make it easier and more plausible—and more scientifically modish—to go on "blaming the victim," a caption which William Ryan has quite appropriately used for his recent important book.[8]

Evaluation research and the controlled field experiment are especially adaptable to studying impacts of specific programs on specific people. They are of little use in studying properties of complex systems which generate and sustain social problems. I am not referring to the system or institution oriented evaluations as described by Suchman, in which "the major function of the evaluator is to help the administrator run his organization in a more effective manner."[9] Rather, the alternative to conventional target impact evaluation which I allude to is the diagnosing of the problem under scrutiny in its relation to the tangled web of structures and processes in the institutional structure within which the problem is found and which apparently sustains the continued existence of the problem, the examination of alternative intervention techniques likewise in terms of their embeddedness within this institutional structure, and their assessment on the basis of informed rational analysis based on what is known about this institutional structure and its relation to the problem.

To repeat, target impact evaluation directs our attention away from these relationships, and is especially designed to keep all of this constant for purposes of analysis, while changing only the intervention variable. Thus it inadvertently minimizes attention to the institutional structure and rivets it on a target population of problem people.

In a recent article, Howard E. Freeman has made a call for renouncing evaluation studies whose outcome variables are normative social indicators or psychological properties, and centering evaluation research

> on universal social systems processes. It must develop criteria that will allow the outcomes of field experiments to be measured in terms of the competence of individuals to negotiate their social environments—criteria that, for want of a better term, will be referred to as *social viability*. [10]

But these words which seem to presage a redirection of evaluation research from the "victim" to the "system" turn out to constitute merely a rearrangement of measuring strategies for assessing the impact of specific intervention programs on problem individuals. "Impact, then," Freeman explains later on, "comes to be measured in terms of the order of individuals before and after an effort has been made to alter them."[11] Thus, despite the reference to systems, the outcome variable is not change in the system, but merely change in rank order of individuals on the outcome variable within the system. Parenthetically, what this indicates is no gain whatsoever for the aggregate of system participants, merely a rearrangement of winners and losers.

A much more widely acknowledged latent effect of evaluation research than its implicit identification of problems as residing in individuals rather than in social systems is the circumstance that evaluation research lends an aura of "science" to the agency's efforts, thus giving it whatever legitimation that aura may carry with it. This may constitute pure ritualism, with such evaluational activity being carried on purely for public relations purposes. But even where it is quite serious, the legitimation issue is an important one.

The question of whether the entire basic intervention strategy is not ill-founded (not merely some of its "aspects" which need improving) does not seem to enter the discussion, even though it might be the best judgment of the researcher on the basis of his research findings combined with informed rational analysis. In such cases, he is thrown into the position of advising the agency to improve a strategy which, however so modified, will in his judgment be ineffective. The situation is only one example of a much larger phenomenon: The latent function of evaluation research—through positive findings or through negative findings which are viewed as suggesting revision or improvement of existing professional technologies and intervention strategies—to support and legitimize the major outlines of agency programs even in the face of continued failure.

In this connection, one should, I believe, reappraise the self-image of evaluation researchers as being in the exciting business of making decisive judgments about the merit of agency programs, and of therefore posing a serious threat to the agencies whose programs are evaluated. To be sure, in the narrower, fragmentalized context of measuring specified impact on a specified population, their potentially negative findings may be highly threatening to the individual program. Caro, for example, writes:

> Implicit in the evaluation role are attempts to discover inefficiency and to encourage change. Administrators, however, usually prefer to conceal inefficiency and resist disruptive change . . . Evaluative researchers are thus predisposed to see a need for change whereas administrators are inclined to defend their efforts and maintain the status quo.[12]

True as this statement is, it applies largely to the narrower, fragmentalized context of measuring specified impact on specified populations. Negative findings may be highly threatening on the level of the individual program with its specific setting and intervention technique. And this possibility or actuality may generate considerable resistance. But the usual implication of evaluation research is not to challenge in any basic way what the agency is doing, but rather to suggest that since the specific isolated program has unsatisfactory impact, it should be modified or substituted by other programs *within the feasibility constraints of the agency involved.*

Hence, evaluation research does not threaten the overall conception of the problem which the agency is seeking to address, nor the agency's overall diagnosis of that problem nor the general professional mode of intervention employed by the agency as this relates to the total social context of the problem. Since the evaluation researcher so often voluntarily limits his deliberations and even his research formulations to the feasibility constraints of the individual agency, he precludes the raising of more important questions as to whether the agency's intervention techniques need more fine-tuning or complete replacement, with an entirely different cast of characters using entirely different intervention techniques. The lesson is all too likely not that the agency should go out of business, but that it needs to "innovate" by making minor incremental modifications in the intervention technique that didn't work, and perhaps to require additional funds in order to work out the imperfections in its presumably basically sound overall approach.

In sum, the latent function of much impact evaluation research is that of reinforcing the major thrust of agency programs, directing attention to problems of fine-tuning of existing intervention strategies and away from causal patterns embedded in the institutional structure, thus reinforcing a conception that agency service approaches are essentially on the "right track" and that the problem lies not with the larger institutional structure or even with the structure of the service system, but primarily with how best to deal with aberrant individuals who are the *real* root of the problem and hence the appropriate target of intervention.

To me, it is a continual source of amazement how unaware research evaluators seem to be of the relation of their own roles, research problem formulations, and research findings, to the social processes in which they find themselves participating and to the larger social processes in which they operate— not as objective Olympians (their own role-perception) but as participants and conscious or inadvertent partisans in a many-sided interplay of juxtaposed interests and conflicting constructions of social reality. The path of escape from the social process through preoccupation with methodological rigor is precluded by the fact that the acceptance of agency problem definitions and the choice of research problems and methodologies carry with them specific theoretical and ideological positions—usually unstated or even unexamined—which have an effect which is parallel to the effect of reporting the specific findings of the evaluation.

Accountability: To Whom, for What?

Running through the above considerations is the larger question of the social context of the evaluation research. Is the setting such that accountability is to those who sponsor or operate the program and thus have a direct interest—not perhaps in the specific program but in the maintenance of the technological approach which the program embodies, and in the general organizational structure and intervention mode in which the organization is engaged? Or is the accountability to a more inclusive system within which not only the specific program but the technological approach, organizational structure, and intervention mode in which the organization is engaged can be put into question, as well as the specific intervention technique being tested?

Most of the literature on evaluation research is based on the first, rather than the second definition of social context. It is designed to help the organization solve its problems within the major outlines of the organization's structure, constituencies, and general modes of intervention. Within these formidable constraints, it assesses the impact effectiveness of this or that specific program. In reviewing the literature assembled in her book of readings, Carol Weiss asserts this fact quite explicitly: "The purpose of evaluation research is to provide information for decision-making about programs "she writes, and she adds that "almost all the authors agree on this."[13]

Alkin puts it even more emphatically:

> Evaluation is the process of ascertaining the decision areas of concern, selecting appropriate information, and collecting and analyzing information in order to report summary data useful to decision-makers in selecting among alternatives.[14]

He goes on to state: "The decision maker, and not the evaluator, determines the nature of the domain to be examined."[15]

Riecken, in discussing program evaluation, states that:

A point on which there is considerable agreement among social scientists who have conducted evaluation studies is that no such study can be successfully executed or its findings utilized in further planning unless the evaluator has been requested by the agency to conduct the study, and, further, unless he has the approval and support of the highest echelon of power in the agency.[16]

Longood and Simmel not only assume that the evaluation researcher will be attached to the organization whose programs he is evaluating, but admonish him to commit himself as a responsible part of that organization. "If he is not willing to share in the responsibility of his organization he himself becomes the principal source of resistance to the innovations which his research may suggest."[17]

Likewise in a book on social research consultation written over a decade ago, I described one of the four roles of the staff social research consultant as "functioning as a member of the administrative team."[18]

But to repeat, the responsibility to the agency whose program is being evaluated, whether the researcher is a staff member of that agency or a contracted evaluator, quite understandably and deliberately delimits the purview of the social scientist's investigations, confining them within the predetermined channel of program decisions made by agency officials. Buchanan, White and Wholey write:

> The evaluator must help the policy maker or program manager to define his information needs and his decision options. Once this is done, the evaluator may discover that the decision-maker needs very basic information about the way his program operates or how services are delivered—not a complex, theoretical model of a social phenomenon, based on tenuous assumptions and limited data.[19]

In moving into the total process at this point, the researcher is usually not asked to make a circumspect scientific attempt at diagnosing the main outlines and dynamics of the problem being addressed, but to address only those aspects of the problem which relate to that particular agency's options for action. As indicated in the quotations just cited, much evaluation research literature tends to suggest that he should do no more. Hence, his potential contribution to the diagnosis of the problem is precluded. Carol Weiss writes, in connection with 10 evaluation research projects funded by NIMH which she studied:

That much evaluation research falls short of the expectations of funders, program staff, and evaluators themselves is due less to limitations of research expertise than to organizational constraints that severely limit the researcher's ability to apply what he knows.[20]

My own opinion is that while this may very well be the case, much of the limitation on the evaluation research is self-imposed.

The issue is well pointed up in a statement by Henry W. Riecken:

Studies of effects represent the maximum contribution that social science can make to social practice, since they are usually intended to feed back results into program planning or policy making.[21]

So long as social scientists confine themselves to diagnoses of problems made implicitly or explicitly by non-social scientists, and so long as they confine their applied efforts to evaluating the impact of fragmented intervention efforts based on such diagnoses, I believe this statement is correct. But of course my whole point is that they should not so confine their efforts and that their contribution will be much greater if they do not.

Alternative Modes of Program Evaluation.

One possible conclusion from what has been said so far would be that evaluation research is admittedly a purely technical function, that it should be ranged under the administration of the agency to be evaluated, that it should be designed to offer useful feedback into the operations of that agency, helping it to make incremental changes in its basic mode of operation. As such, it should stay away from larger social problem diagnoses and should stay away from theoretical preoccupations, except as these may have direct bearing on the program options presently feasible for the given agency.

I believe that this is a quite tenable position from the standpoint both of agency executives who want to make minor modifications to improve their programs, and from the standpoint of evaluation researchers who see themselves essentially as research technicians and are not concerned with the relation of the agency's efforts to the total configuration of the social problem under consideration but rather with whether the agency's program is making a dent on some indicator believed relevant to the problem under consideration.

But the position has three unavoidable consequences.

First, it does relegate the evaluation researcher to the position of a research technician rather than of a scientist with substantive knowledge to contribute.

Second, it limits his efforts to the constraints of the agency situation—its constraints involving funding, technical competence, feasibility, magnitude of effort, availability of resources, and so on, and to what that agency under those constraints can do with regard to a specific problem.

Third, it does much to vitiate the notion of great actual and potential impact of social science on social policy. The major questions of social policy are not questions of how this or that agency should make minor modifications in its programs, but whether entire program complexes and strategies are appropriate to the nature of the problems, or whether quite different alternatives should be pursued. These questions are not at present and may never be amenable to solution through controlled field experiments. If social scientists are to address these questions, they must therefore employ not just impact research design but what I have called informed rational analysis, including what is known from a social theory, from agency practice, and from previous social science research on the topic—not only evaluation research.

There are, it seems to be, two options for pertinent contributions by social scientists in addressing these larger evaluative questions. The first is the more serious and concentrated effort to apply social science analysis to larger policy evaluation questions. While specific research evaluation findings may constitute part of the intellectual resources available for such efforts, these reports are, in a sense, more important in their aggregate patterns than in their individual findings. For they add up to disciplined experience from which conclusions can be drawn about the likelihood of future impact not only of those specific interventions but of entire classes of interventions within which incremental variations might be introduced. Putting this another way, not every bit of inferior ore need be extracted from a vein before the prospector makes a reasoned judgment that the vein is no longer worth pursuing. We should look to social scientists for help in locating other more promising veins of exploration rather than only for help in trying more efficiently to exploit these poor veins.

In this connection, there are some specific lines of endeavor suggested in the statement by Carol Weiss that: "Little is done to apply existing theory and knowledge to program development, to study means for securing acceptance of new programs, or to analyze alternative methods for their implementation with bureaucratic structures."22

These suggestions relate to the agency and program level, but they indicate a broader and more imaginative contribution than simply that of assessing the impact of programs formulated by others.

But there is another option as well. This would be for social scientists to insist on a broader scope in their research evaluations. They would make full use of controlled field experiments in evaluation research where this is appropriate. But they could also insist on examining as well the presuppositions on which the intervention strategy is formulated. They could be concerned with the social context of evaluation research not merely in terms of how the research can actually be carried out and how the utilization of findings by the agency can be increased, but in the broader analysis of where the program and the evaluation effort fit within the social structure surrounding the substantive problem area.

It would be presumptuous to claim at this point to be able to delineate all the dimensions of what a more thorough and circumspect and analytic approach based on social science would be to the problem of evaluating a specific intervention strategy, over and beyond conventional evaluation research technology. But a number of considerations can be mentioned which might be included in any such broadly based evaluation.

1. The evaluator can seek to gather what is known or hypothesized in the social sciences about the nature of the problem which is being addressed by the intervention strategy to be evaluated.

2. He can then examine, assuming that the intervention strategy accomplishes the desired specific impact, whether and in what way the existence of the problem would be affected.

3. He can become quite clear in his mind whether the intervention strategy is designed to prevent the problem, to remove the problem in individual cases, or to alleviate it.

4. Depending on his understanding of which of these is being attempted in the intervention, he can spend considerable

effort in reviewing whether in his best scientific judgment the intervention strategy is appropriate to the anticipated objective; whether there is sufficient reason for anticipating that the desired impact will ensue.

5. He can also consider whether, in the light of existing knowledge and experience, other intervention techniques might more reasonably be expected to attain the same objective with less investment of resources or a greater impact with an equivalent investment of resources.

6. If through informed rational analysis he assesses the effort to be of little potential value, simply wasteful, or worse, a mere deception, he can make this opinion clear. On an ethical basis, I would add that in such cases he should seriously consider advising that the project not be undertaken; and if it is undertaken, he should seriously consider withholding his own participation from it, unless he is already contractually obligated by the time he reaches this decision—a situation to be avoided if possible.

7. In considering advising that the project not be undertaken, or in considering his own nonparticipation, he should entertain the possibility that he is wrong in his own assessment. This is not easy, but it is difficult to see how a man of principle can escape the issue. He does not escape it by simply agreeing to participate in any or all evaluation projects for which he is offered an inducement—since this itself is a position on the issue.

8. He can form some opinion as to the political feasibility factors involved in implementing such a program on an appropriately broad scale, if found effective.

9. He can consider the consequences which might be anticipated if the program is found effective through the impact evaluation and is expanded into general usage throughout the appropriate target populations. This relates to possible side effects, and to trying to identify possible consequences which otherwise would remain unidentified until after the intervention program is put into broad usage.

10. He can take into consideration the relation of this program to other programs addressed to or affecting the same social problem. Is the relationship mutually supportive, zero-sum, or what, as to their joint effects?

11. He can consider who benefits from the program in addition to the assumed eventual benefit to the target popula-

tion. As examples, does he benefit? Do other researchers? Does the agency? Does the taxpayer? Other agencies? Other groups or categories of people? And by the same token, who pays— and in what ways? For example, who pays monetarily, in terms of where the funds come from? But in addition, what social costs are involved? For whom?

These suggestions are indicative of possible facets of a more broadly based approach by social scientists, and by professional practitioners as well, to the evaluation function. They do not exhaust the possibilities. Others not mentioned may be still more appropriate. They reflect not a denial of the controlled field experiment approach to program impact evaluation, but rather a need for its supplementation by other evaluative methods if the findings of social scientists are to be put in adequate perspective as a basis for program and policy decisions—not only of the individual agencies, but of the complex society in which they operate.

Footnotes for Chapter 1

[1] Howard E. Freeman, "Outcome Measures and Social Acxperiments: An Immodest Proposal for Redirecting Research Efforts," *The American Sociologist*, Vol. 7, No. 9 (November 1972), p. 17.

[2] Peter H. Rossi, "Practice, Method, and Theory in Evaluating Social-Action Programs," Chapter 10 in James L. Sundquist, ed., *On Fighting Poverty.* New York: Basic Books, Inc., 1969, p. 225.

[3] Carol Weiss, "The Politicization of Evaluation Research," *Journal of Social Issues*, Vol. 26, No. 4 (Autumn 1970), p. 67. Reprinted in her *Evaluating Action Programs: Readings in Social Action and Education*, Boston: Allyn and Bacon, Inc., 1972.

[4] Egon G. Guba, "The Failure of Educational Evaluation." *Educational Technology, Vol. 9, No. 5, 1969, reprinted in Carol H. Weiss, Evaluation Action Programs: Readings in Social Action and Education*, p. 263. Italics added.

[5] Roland L. Warren, "A Multi-problem Confrontation," in Gordon E. Brown, ed., *The Multi-Problem Dilemma: A Social Research Demonstration with Multi-Problem Families*, Metuchen, N. J.: The Scarecrow Press, Inc., 1968, p. 88.

[6] *Op.*, p. 220.

[7] "The Politicization of Evaluation Research," p. 60.

[8] William Ryan, *Blaming the Victim*, New York: Pantheon Books, 1971.

[9] Edward A. Suchman, "Action for What? A Critique of Evaluation Research." in *Evaluating Action Programd: Readings in Social Action and Education*, p. 76.

[10] Howard E. Freeman, *op, cit.*

[11] *Ibid.*

[12] Francis G. Caro, ed., *Readings in Evaluation Research*. New York: Russell Sage Foundation, 1971, pp. 14-15.

[13] *Ibid.*, p. 18.

[14] Marvin C. Alkin, "Evaluation Theory Development," *Evaluation Comment*, Vol. 2, No. 1 (October 1969), reprinted in *Evaluating Action Programs: Readings in Social Action and Education*, p. 107.

[15] *Ibid.*

[16] Henry W. Riecken, "Memorandum on Program Evaluation," Internal memorandum to the Ford Foundation, October 1953, reprinted in *Evaluating Action Programs: Readings in Social Action and Education*, pp. 98-99.

[17] Robert Longwood and Arnold Simmel, "Organizational Resistance to Innovation Suggested by Research," paper presented at the 1962 meeting of the American Sociological Association, reprinted in *Evaluating Action Programs: Readings in Social Action and Education*, p. 317.

[18] Roland L. Warren, *Social Research Consultation: An Experiment in Health and Welfare Planning*. New York: Russell Sage Foundation, 1963, p. 43.

[19] Garth N. Buchanan, Bayla F. White and Joseph S. Wholey, "Political Considerations in the Design of Program Evaluation," paper presented at 1971 meeting of American Sociological Association. Mimeographed. The Urban Institute, Washington, D. C., p. 3.

[20] Carol H. Weiss, *Organizational Constraints on Evaluative Research*, New York: Columbia University Bureau of Applied Social Research, 1971, p. 1.

[21] *Op. cit.*, p. 86.

[22] "The Politicization of Evaluation Research," *op. cit.*, pp. 65-66.

COMMENTARY

Joseph W. Eaton

Social Aspects of Methodology

Evaluation requires a methodology. It also is a social and political activity to which Roland L. Warren's thought-provoking chapter is addressed. Little controversy among qualified specialists is possible about the representativeness of a sample that might be used in an evaluative study. Its administrative utility, social value or political context involve more normative criteria.

Professor Warren quotes Howard Freeman that "we are moving in the direction of becoming an experimental society." When viewed in a historical context this viewpoint is compelling. There is widespread acceptance of the theory that man need not be passive about his future. He can plan for it.

At the personal level, it takes the form of career planning, the purchase of life insurance or the making of a will. There also are investments and loans, so that money is used in the present to be paid off through anticipated future earnings.

At the social level, the Social Security and Medicare programs protect large segments of the population against pauperization. The future is not left to chance.

Positive Negativism

The effectiveness of these plans, personal *and* social, generally falls short of what is expected of them by those who made them. Professor Warren stresses the frequently negative outcomes of evaluative research studies.

Outcomes are most likely to be negative when researchers adopt single criteria. Group counselling as well as work and study programs in prisons have not yet been shown to contribute much to the reduction of recidivism after felons are discharged. But the findings are much more positive when measured against such criteria as evidence of humanistic interactions among convicts and staff or a prison's capacity to recruit and keep guards who are interested in transforming prisons into therapeutic as well as custodial institutions.[1]

[1] Joseph W. Eaton, *Stonewalls Not a Prison Make*, Springfield, Ill., Charles C. Thomas, 1963.

One also needs to consider the positive consequences of negative findings. There has been no diminution of cancer research in spite of the frequent evidence that turns out to be unproductive for helping us learn how cancer might be prevented or controlled. Each experiment which fails to yield the hoped-for outcome permits future investigators to try different approaches. But as Professor Warren points out negative findings are often interpreted in the applied social sciences, as warranting abandonment of a theoretically promising lead. This attitude is less common in medical and engineering research.

Social scientists need more public support for the idea that demonstrations of insufficient impact of a social technique cannot always justify that it be abandoned. Child Guidance Clinics fail to reach many of their clients. But would this justify their being closed? The problems they treat will continue to exist. Negative findings must become challenges to better, more innovative programing.

Not enough executives of social agencies feel secure enough in their jobs and in their knowledge to react to negative findings as an opportunity to obtain sanctions to try out new ideas. So many agencies conform to the generalization presented by Professor Warren. They oppose genuine evaluative research.

The Role Of
Social Strategy

This fact suggests that evaluative researchers need to add some methodological skills that are outside the range of their conventional training programs in research methods and in statistics. They must study techniques of organizational strategy. Findings must so be presented that there is an encouragement of social forces favorable to their utilization. A pathologist who finds that a misdiagnosis led to failure of a surgical operation, even if the patient dies, will not bring about the public criticism or disbarment of the physician, unless there was gross negligence. Evaluative research findings in social work, in education and in social medicine must be presented with similar respect for the work situation of social practitioners. Their knowledge always falls short of what is needed to achieve a high degree of control. But their concern with social programming is likely to bring about results in excess of what would be produced by chance or the total absence of planned social action.

Evaluation cannot be a matter of dichotomous judgments— good or bad, expensive or cheap, effective or ineffective. A social operation can be judged by multiple criteria. Outcomes always differ, depending on which one of several multiple criteria is applied.

Let us return to penology—a field of social practice where we seem to be fighting many losing battles. In highly urbanized societies, violent crime and other law violations often increase in spite of common efforts to develop remedial programs. Prevention of crime is not the only criterion of effectiveness. other relevant criteria are help to victims from unnecessary suffering, greater speed and lower cost of admin- istration of justice, maintaining an organizational climate favorable to critical analysis of ideas of what might be done to reduce crime or to limit its damage to those who survive it.

Evaluative researchers must be satisfied with modest increments in the probability of social benefit. Dramatic reversals of unpleasant effects are uncommon, in part because of what Peter Rossi stated so well elsewhere. Most social programs are built upon others, which may already have done a good deal to affect the problem—as is the case with compulsory primary school education. Within most schools youngsters learn how to read, write and many other basic skills. What is left for new programming often conforms to Professor Warren's assertion: "What is left is the possibility of only marginal improvements at high cost." (p. 26 of the article).

The Curicular Effect
Mechanism

Evaluative research findings must be interpreted with regard to the well known fact that there is social relationship between evidence and the persons who use it. An optimistic finding that group counselling works to some extent, encour- ages those who use it and makes the public more inclined to try it. Further, negative findings discourage both and may even lead to premature abandonment of a practice which could well have value, but needs to be improved rather than abandoned.

The social-psychological relationship betwen data and people is not always kept in view by those who engage in evaluative research and who then report their findings, expecting that they be treated with the finality of a Supreme Court ruling. This "holier than thou" attitude, as Professor Warren calls it, will not disappear simply by being attacked as disfunctional to the purposes for which evaluative research is usually undertaken. It is rooted in the way we train social scientists in most of our colleges and universities.

The Relevancy Criterion

When the design of a study is good, the researcher can feel secure from having his capabilities questioned by peers. But evaluative research often has to be done with methodological short-comings. This fact subjects the work to lower scientific status. Many evaluative studies must be cheap enough to be done. The result must become available in sufficient time to have practitical utility for those who want them. Evaluative researchers must include relevancy, along with reliability and validity as criteria for estimating the social significance of what they do. There are statistical tests for reliability and validity, but not for relevancy. This makes the latter a more controversial criterion.

Evaluative researchers therefore need to pay much attention to the impact of their social role on practitioners. As Professor Warren sums up—they must also be aware of whom they're accountable for, what they do, for what purposes and with what impact on the larger system in which the practice occurs in which they are studying.

Conclusion

Anyone concerned with the advancement of evaluative research must recognize that this process is most likely to be utilized when the ideology of programs and of agencies includes evaluation as one of the criteria of what justified the attribution of quality. There is more and more evidence that attention is being paid to this concept. Federal funding agencies generally demand more than data on the professional qualifications of the staff and the methods used in a program. They also wish to be informed about what measures have been adopted to engage in evaluative research.

Social science departments in the better universities are not yet well prepared to train the specialists needed for the performance of this function. Students would be required to study with as much systematic attention the organizational variables of doing research in an action agency, as may now be devoted to some more abstract features of the curriculum. Professor Warren ends his essay with a formulation of eleven "commandments". I would add a twelfth:

The researcher must examine his findings to see how they can be used to estimate the alternate probabilities of keeping a present practice, of changing it, or of abandoning it as probably irrelevant.

Evaluative research is likely to gain much more social acceptance when outcomes are measured on the basis of modest incremental effects rather than against the expectation of an occasional dramatic fundamental discovery. Evaluative research results must be applied with the awareness that plausible leads deserve being explored.

In these explorations, we must guard against the positive bias of *newism*. It is an ideology which equates newness with betterness. Tradition or the status quo are seen as negative. Novelty is presumed to be a good index of validity.

Merchandising relies much on newism in marketing its products. New model cars are always advertised as being better than older models. Some of the innovations may indeed be safer, cleaner or more economical. But there also may be unanticipated manufacturing, design and inspection errors. By the time testing and consumer use uncovers such problems in new models, the public has already purchased them and is ready for a later version.

But newism also has functions that serve to enhance the development of genuinely improved programs. The ideology helps to enhance the status of practitioners who are trying something new as "innovators." When experimentation is socially encouraged, and evaluative research monitors are the outcome, genuine improvements are likely to be made.

The history of the applied social sciences includes much more than what men were able to prove conclusively. It also is influenced by social dynamics. Newism, in the short run, can lead to faddish shifts in practices, but it is also a major factor in maintaining a social climate of support of serious practitioners who are ready to replace unsatisfactory programs with as yet unproven but promising ideas. What differentiates the diletante from the genuine innovator is concern with utilizing evaluative research data in making final determinations about the use of alternate social practices.

CHAPTER 2

The Political Context of Evaluation

James G. Coke
John E. Hansan

In recent years, evaluation research has emerged as a self-conscious activity. Yet we might remind ourselves that politics has always included an evaluative component. The decisions of politicians are based upon judgments about the past or anticipated future effectiveness of programs and agencies. Like the Frenchman who was surprised to discover that he had always been speaking prose, politicians might be surprised to be told that they are program evaluators.

Political theory has traditionally assumed that the most effective evaluation occurs as a matter of course through the ordinary processes of representative democracy. In this view, legislators are thought to be especially appropriate evaluators, and the legislative institution the most effective means of carrying out continuing evaluation. Democratic ideology assumes that *vox populi, vox dei.* It therefore follows that those who are chosen by the people possess evaluative insights that are, at least in part, divinely inspired. Periodic elections and the feedback of information from constituents assure popular accountability and responsiveness in the evaluation process.

If evaluation has always been an integral part of the political process, and if legislative evaluations are presumed to have the highest validity, why, then, have we recently turned to other modes of evaluation, and why have we tended to give evaluation a separate identity, apart from politics.

Several forces in modern society create a presumption that evaluation can and should be separated from politics. One is the putative power of scientific analysis, which has produced such activities as PPB, cost-effectiveness studies, operation research, and systems analysis. All these inventions hold forth the potential of substituting hard, verifiable data for intuitive, subjective impressions as a basis for public decision-making. At its worst, the lure of scientific analysis can lull us into believing that if we simply gather enough data and subject them to sophisticated manipulation, the results will somehow speak for themselves, thereby removing the necessity for making any decisions at all. In either case, "science" has a much more positive connotation to the modern mind than "politics." The modern mind is suspicious of politics, perhaps because of its unsystematic character.

A second reason for the separation of evaluation from politics is that many believe that legislative institutions have atrophied. In addition to being untrustworthy, legislatures are said to be ineffective. The executive branch monopolizes information and expertise. The "best and the brightest" also gravitate toward service in the executive branch, where they can achieve power much faster than in seniority-dominated legislative systems. Because of these factors, the legislature tends to become a veto group, rather than the initiator of policies for the executive branch to administer. Even those who have recently come to appreciate the innovative role of individual legislators[1] still recognize the short-comings of the performance of the legislature as a body.

A third reason is intergovernmental suspicion. In the human service arena, as in most others, the federal government has stimulated the widespread introduction of new programs. But the federal government does not operate them. Because of the decentralized nature of the American political system, the federal role has been restricted to financial assistance and standard-setting through categorical, conditional, matching grants. Local and state governments, and occasionally non-profit groups, are the actual administrators of federal programs. The national groups and coalitions that successfully promote federal involvement in human service programs tend to be very suspicious of local and state governments. This suspicion is not without foundation. Local and state governments have so many constraints on their operations that they have a very limited capacity to innovate. Therefore, evaluation research becomes a way of enforcing accountability in intergovernmental relations, especially when the higher level of government seeks to change program routines at the lower levels through the leverage of project grants.

Sometimes evaluation research is particularly important in human service arenas that are redistributive in nature. Redistributive issues, which are those that affect the relative power of social classes, are hard to handle in the American political system; they tend to be converted into distributive issues.[2] That is, public programs tend to be disaggregated so that everyone can get a piece of the action. Evaluation research can be one part of a funding agency's strategy to assure itself that redistributive goals are not being subverted by local and state administration.

It is somewhat ironic that essentially political factors rising out of intergovernmental relations, the role of the legislature, and the presumed nonpartisanship of science should have generated a movement to substitute scientific evaluation research for the judgments of political leaders. Yet those same political processes frustrate scientific evaluation by producing sets of objectives in most human service programs that are not framed so as to facilitate the type of experimental evaluation that is most in accord with social science methods. In the words of Robert Weiss and Martin Rein, human service programs have "broad aims and unstandardized forms."[3] As stated in legislation and administrative guidelines, the various objectives of a program are frequently vague and usually inconsistent. Multiplicity, ambiguity, and inconsistency are inherent in the legislative and administrative process.

The process of legislation encourages each specialized group to place its imprint on what may originally have been a straightforward, uncomplicated proposal. Different facets are stressed by the different groups, so that the original idea may emerge from the end of the legislative pipeline in highly altered and embellished form. Each group molds the product: legislative sponsors, the bureaucracies responsible for administration, professional elites, clients, and constituents (who may or may not be also clients). In a sense, each interested group takes away a special measuring rod by which to judge the subsequent effectiveness of the program.

These measuring rods may be applied to inputs, to outputs, or to outcomes.[4] Some legislators will be pleased with the minimization of negative outcomes on important constituencies; others stress the achievement of intended positive results. Since program operators are usually concerned most with procedural inputs, the bureaucracies responsible for the program will emphasize the relative ease of administration. Professional elites will most frequently try to relate objectives to outcomes, while constituents are usually the least concerned with the gap between legislative and executive decisions and their implementation.

Most significant, perhaps, is the fact that programs can be

merely a legislative response to a public demand to do something about what is, at base, an insoluble problem. Human service programs, like many others, may be placebos—ways to mollify angry groups or to show that we are concerned. As the popular phrase goes, there ought to be a law. And, in America, there usually is. Edward C. Banfield identifies the two categorical imperatives that seem to guide much public action in the United States: (1) "Don't just sit there. Do something!" and (2) "Do good!"[5] The result is legislation that creates what political scientists sometimes refer to as symbolic outcomes. Yet a major social myth on which democratic systems operate is that public sector actions should have real outcomes, not just symbolic ones.

In such a political context, it may be very misleading to rely heavily upon the results of scientific evaluation that follows the canons of the newer, rigorous research methodologies. Programs often change in subtle ways during the course of an evaluation. Astute administrators anticipate the reactions of clients, constituents, and legislators, and quietly shift the emphasis among the diverse objectives that constitute the ostensible aims of the program. Older agencies have an institutional memory that allows for change with a minimum of overt conflict. Evaluators may not recognize that the organization has evolved into a different one, in which the pre-test, post-test model of evaluation cannot apply.

The vague and inconsistent quality of legislatively-mandated objectives may produce an insuperable initial difficulty. The evaluator does not know which objective is to be primary, or whether one objective is to be stressed over others in a sequential manner. A good example of this inherent dilemma in evaluation is the proverty program. There were two major objectives: maximum feasible participation of the groups to be served, and coordination of services. Was participation to have primacy over coordination? Or was one of the objectives to be stressed first, and then the other? These are all unknown, and therefore the evaluation job is logically impossible.[6]

Even if objectives were to be clear and consistent, there is a particular characteristic of the American political system that inhibits evaluation. This is the administration of human service programs by hundreds of state and local governments, each of which imbeds any human services program in its own peculiar political process. Thus, there are literally thousands of meanings to any given program. It is not really possible to evaluate against universal criteria in such a system. A single program may have widely diverse meanings for the participants in various community contexts. An example is the variation in Community Action programs in Ohio between rural and urban areas. It appears that the rural CAP programs have assumed the role of a centralized planning operation within the county, filling the void of professional competence in such community systems. It would be fruitless to evaluate such a program against the explicit goals of the 1964 Economic Opportunity Act or other national objectives, which might be more applicable to the complex and specialized community decision-making systems usually found in urban areas.

Thus, by providing programs with multiple, vaguely-stated goals and by introducing a bias toward local administration of national programs, the American political context greatly reduces the utility of scientific evaluation, especially of the type that utilizes experimental design. Quite apart from the political context, the evaluation enterprise is inherently tainted by what Walter Williams calls "the iron law of absolute evaluation flaws," that is, "the absolute methodological and logistical deficiencies in any evaluation (which) make political infighting a near certainty when evaluation results threaten a popular program."[7]

The clear implication of this overview of the political context is that evaluation and politics are inextricably intertwined, despite the ideology and good intentions that would seek to separate them. Indeed, the technology of evaluation— its design, methods, and procedures—has no meaning unless it is embedded in a political decision-making process.

The most important methodological inventions will be those that integrate evaluation with decision-making. The most useful debate over method and technique is over their administrative utility. For example, Carol Weiss suggests that evaluators should identify latent goals—"such as showing that the administration was 'doing something,' placating powerful interest groups, enhancing the influence of a particular division or department"—and measure on these dimensions.[8] In short, Weiss asks that evaluators lay bare a social myth and recognize that some programs are not designed to produce real outcomes. Some would disagree with this suggestion, but if one pursues the logic of experimental design relentlessly, it is a reasonable technique. Whether it would be administratively useful is another matter, and is a legitimate subject for debate.

A basic issue in the integration of evaluation with decision-making is the specificity of program planning. Evaluation is now linked up with a type of planning that goes much farther than setting directions. Planning, as Robert Levine points out, now means a detailed specification of objectives and optimal courses to reach them. It is in the nature of these systems to fail, says Levine, because their implementation is governed by the cumulation of partial failures.[9] This type of planning "fits" with experimental evaluation design. It is possible, however, to redefine planning to answer the question "In what direction do we want to go?" *not* "Where do we want to get?"[10] If planning becomes directional, rather than oriented to end-states, this would fit with nonexperimental methodologies. Robert Weiss and Martin Rein call for the development of just such methodologies, so that evaluation research would become "concerned with describing the unfolding form of the experimental intervention, the reactions of individuals and institutions subjected to its impact, and the consequences, so far as they can be learned by interview and observation, for these individuals and institutions . . . . it would be much more concerned with learning than with measuring."[11] And it would clearly be more relevant to policy development.

In its broader sense, the evaluation enterprise is carried on by several types of actors: political philosophers, legislators, and executives. For any actor, the political context ultimately gives meaning to the evaluative role. Walter Williams cogently expresses this fact in his description of the central analyst, who is an especially important evaluator:

> The analyst is neither pure politican nor pure scientist. He probably should have at his fingertips both *The Prince* and a text on principles of experimental design, and use both of them. As an analyzer of programs, he must function as a skeptic; this surely makes him different from a program operator. But he has to decide what to analyze and what information to generate in support of analysis. Seldom is this decision determined on technical grounds alone; methodological concerns generally will only delimit boundaries because some approaches are technically infeasible. A choice, however, such as that made in

the Head Start evaluation, clearly rests on value judgments. The analyst's choices ultimately depend on his value judgments about what is important and on his bureaucratic/political judgments about where policy analysis will have the most impact (that is, where the weak points in the policy process are).[12]

Footnotes for Chapter 2

[1] See, for example, Frederic N. Cleaveland and Associates, *Congress and Urban Problems* (Washington, D. C.: The Brookings Institution, 1969).

[2] For the distinction among regulatory, distributive, and redistributive issues, see Theodore J. Lowi, "American Business, Public Policy Case Studies, and Political Theory," *"World Politics*, Vol. 16 (July, 1964), pp. 677-715.

[3] Robert S. Weiss and Martin Rein, "The Evaluation of Broad-Aim Programs: A Cautionary Case and a Moral," *The Annals*, Vol. 385 (September, 1969), p. 134.

[4] Outcomes are the consequences of outputs, which may be intended or unintended.

[5] Edward C. Banfield, *The Unheavenly City* (Boston: Little, Brown and Company, 1970), p. 249.

[6] This point is discussed by Edward Banfield in the useful symposium entitled "Nixon, The Great Society, and The Future of Social Policy," *Commentary*, Vol. 55, No. 5 (May, 1973, pp. 31-61.

[7] Walter Williams, *Social Policy Research and Analysis: The Experience in the Federal Social Agencies* (New York: American Elsevier Publishing Co., 1971), p. 123.

[8] Carol H. Weiss, "The Politics of Impact Measurement," *Policy Studies Journal*, Vol. 1, No. 3 (Spring, 1973), p. 181. This is a very cogent article dealing with the same themes as those in this paper.

[9] Robert A. Levine, *Public Planning: Failure and Redirection*(New York: Basic Books, 1972).

[10] *Ibid.*, pp. 162-167.

[11] Weiss and Rein, *op. cit.*, p. 142.

[12] W. Williams, *op. cit.*, pp. 170-171.

COMMENTARY

Joe R. Hoffer

One must agree with the authors that evaluative research and politics are extricably intertwined, despite the ideology and good intentions that would seek to separate them. Furthermore, that technology of evaluation—its design, methods and procedures—has no meaning unless it is embedded in a political decision- making process.

And yet, there are ample examples that evaluative research outside the political arena has not only produced objective data which have influenced decisions by administrators and legislators but also have contributed to a more informed citizenry.

The authors in a much too brief narrative highlight some of the obstacles and problems facing social scientist evaluators in working within the political system and imply many others.

Within the legislative branch of government, powerful legislators, legislative committees, and their staffs have important input into the composition of each bill. In the executive branch, again, there are a number of actors—the bureaus and their staff, the Office of Management and Budget and the White House.

The final bill as may be expected from any collective action usually defines the objectives of the program in broad terms and these objectives may be inconsistent. Even if the objectives were to be clear and consistent, the authors point out that the administration of human services programs is performed by hundreds of state and local governmental units and thereby greatly reduces the utility experimental design. Furthermore, Sharkansky reminds us that the constitutional structure of federalism helps to protect the interests of state governments, but does not protect institutions of local governments from either federal or state governments.[1] The purpose and nature of federal grants and the requirements that come along with the money are frequent sources of conflicts between federal, state and local administrators and the social science evaluator is caught in these conflicts.

There are many actors on the state and national levels and the local scene is no exception; special interest groups, elected officials and administrators are essential ingredients in our

democratic society. Nevertheless, they have conflicting political interests and concerns and thereby increase the difficulty
of rational decision-making. In addition to the political implications, there is another factor that we must consider in defining
a role of evaluative research and that is that federal, state and
local administrators represent a wide range of professions and
not each member of a profession has a common professional
view of the world. There are different schools of thought
within each profession. These may and do generate disputes
among the members of one profession within an agency at the
same time that other disputes occur between the members of
different professions. This factor is not conducive to social
science researchers in contributing to the improvement of
political decisions.

Notwithstanding these impressive obstacles to effective
evaluative research, Rivlin reminds us that "although the
problem of who should be benefited is clearly a political
problem, the analyst can still help by indicating the consequences in benefit-cost terms, of attaching different weights to
the benefits flowing to various groups."[2]

In recent years, administrators and legislative bodies have
been appealing to social scientists to help concerning the
effectiveness of existing programs and for assistance in
determining what kinds of policies, facilities and personnel to
employ.

One example of efforts in this direction has been the
Planning, Programming and Budgeting System (PPBS). This
system was devised in 1961 by the Secretary of Defense, Robert
S. McNamara. The system was devised as a means of providing
policy-makers with an analytic evaluation of existing and
proposed programs, buttressed wherever possible with quantitative measures of performance. In 1965, President Johnson
directed that PPBS be adopted by the civilian agencies of the
federal government in the preparation of their budget requests. Today with the infusion of management technicians on
all administrative and policy levels of human services programs, there is a resurgence of efforts to implement this
system.

PPBS is a subtle and alluring system that appears to offer a
Utopia. True, it has been used successfully by the Pentagon
and the National Aeronautics and Space Administration, but
both these agencies operate in a subject area in which costs/

benefits and end results can be easily determined. For obvious reasons, PPBS has not been an overwhelming success in government departments dealing primarily with human relations services.

PPBS groups under one rubric similar problems or functions to make comparisons of objectives and programs and thereby determine which is most effective. When programs are dispersed throughout various agencies, this is difficult to accomplish. For example, in the federal government today, education is administered in forty different agencies. The same difficulty exists with most social problems, such as delinquency, poverty, family breakdown, racism, and so on. PPBS is essentially a framework for planning—a way of organizing information and analysis in a systematic fashion so that the consequences of practical choices can be seen clearly. This is a fine idea, but most difficult to achieve.

Another requirement is that costs must be estimated for the various alternatives for one and five-year periods. This requirement, while it can be met, will be resisted by the human service professions because of its difficulty of achievement.

Finally, a major requirement of PPBS is the evaluation of benefits or costs/benefits. In the absence of suitable criteria or social indicators, it represents the greatest obstacle to be overcome if PPBS is to make a major contribution in social welfare. But these difficulties should not deter the human service professions from applying the basic ingredients of PPBS to our hard-core problems. We have some experience with systems analysis. The very process of analysis is valuable in itself, for it will force us to think about the real objectives of our programs and how they can be measured.

Finally, if PPBS is to survive as a system, it must fit into the political process and at the same time must modify that process. Schultz suggests the view "that the effectiveness, and indeed survival, of PPBS will depend on recognizing, but not slavishly following, political constraints in the selection of issues to be examined and alternatives to be considered. The severity of those constraints," he concludes, "varies substantially from program to program, although not in a completely unpredictable way."[3]

Both Hitch[4] and Schultze[5] argued cogently that government should make decisions as systematically as possible— arraying alternative policies, assembling information on the advantages and disadvantages of each, and estimating the costs and benefits of public action. From their analysis of such tools of systematic decision-making as program budgets, multi-year plans, and program memoranda, Hitch and Schultze conclude that two major messages come through: (1) it is better to have some idea where you are going than to fly blind, and (2) it is better to be orderly than haphazard about decision-making.

These messages should provide social science researchers ample operating room—to be separated from politics and at the same time to become embedded in a political decision-making process.

Footnotes for Commentary

[1] Ira Sharkansky, *Public Administration: Policy-Making in Government Agencies.* Chicago: Markham Publishing Company, 1968, p. 238.

[2] Alice M. Rivlin, *Systematic Thinking for Social Action*, Washington, D. C.: The Brookings Institution, 1971, p. 58.

[3] Charles L. Schultze, *The Politics and Economics of Public Spending.* (Washington, D. C.: The Brookings Institution, 1968), p. 101.

[4] Charles J. Hitch, *Decision-Making for Defence.* (Berkeley, California: University of California Press, 1965).

[5] Charles L. Schultze, *Op. Cit.*

CHAPTER 3

The Organizational Context of Evaluation:
When Norms of Validity Fail to Guide
Gate-Keeping Decisions in Service Organizations

Saad Z. Nagi

Aside from general policies concerned with distribution of resources, the mechanisms for society's coping with such social problems as illness, disability, family disorganization, unemployment, lack of skills, illiteracy, and poverty, may be grouped into three categories: (a) norms to guide the behavior of persons in question and the expectations of others; (b) knowledge, techniques, and professions to combat the problems and alleviate their consequences; and (c) organizations through which professionals and others apply relevant knowledge and techniques in assisting those who need services and benefits. The effectiveness of policies and programs directed to social problems, then, depends in large measure upon access and interaction of consumers of services with agencies and professionals who provide them.

Service and benefit relations of applicants to organizations begin by assuming the status of clients or beneficiaries. A person becomes a client of a given service organization as the culmination of a number of steps and decisions, some of which are undertaken by, or on behalf of, applicants. The change from applicant to client depends on certain of the organization's decisions and actions, which are generally intended to establish eligibility for the services sought. Most organizations set qualifications or requirements as criteria for eligibility. However, not all persons who are eligible for the various services apply for them, nor do all applicants qualify for the services they seek. Organizations vary in the decision processes of "gate-keeping"—determining whether or not an applicant is eligible for given services or benefits.

This paper is primarily addressed to gate-keeping decisions. First, I will describe the patterns of gate-keeping decisions, and identify important factors that affect them. I will conclude by attempting to discern some of the consequences when norms of validity fail to guide decisions, and the patterns of decision making and client-organization relations that evolve.

Patterns Of Gate-Keeping Decisions

Unlike decisions involved in optimizing profits, in reaching agreements in political negotiations, or in the selection of treatment modalities for clients already admitted to services, alternatives in gate-keeping decisions in service organizations are similar to legal decisions and are often termed "quasi-judicial." These decisions are primarily oriented to establishing the "rights" of applicants and determining their "entitlement" to services or benefits for which they apply. An applicant is either defined as eligible and thus becomes a client or a beneficiary of an organization, or he is found ineligible and is denied services and benefits. True, some organizations may refer applicants to other organizations, and in the rare case organizations exist whose sole function is to make referrals. But the alternative choices in screening decisions are generally limited to the acceptance or rejection of applicants.

The processes of judicial or quasi-judicial decision making are built around the development of *criteria*, the collection of *evidence*, and the exercise of *judgment* in applying criteria to evidence. For decisions in service organizations, laws are supplemented by rules and regulations of the organizations themselves. It is significant that most service organizations have *both* the power to set criteria on eligibility by formulating rules on the provision of services and benefits, and to decide on the acceptance or rejection of applicants. As will become more evident, these two powers may be used by organizations in adapting to their environments, at times even defeating the interests of the clients.

Two major types of decision processes can be identified. The first is based upon objectively defined criteria for which there are concrete indicators, as in the case of decisions on eligibility for medicare coverage or retirement benefits upon reaching a certain age. Such decisions are of a *routine* nature and only entail a mechanical matching of simple evidence with clear-cut criteria. When the evidence called for is not available, designating an acceptable substitute has also become fairly routinized.

The second type of decision processes, which may be called *non-routine*, entails judgment on the nature of evidence to be collected and on the application of criteria to evidence.

Examples of the non-routine decisions are individual and family services, admissions to hospitals and clinics, entitlement for disability compensation and benefits, and the provision of rehabilitation services. A complex set of factors needs to be considered in determining eligibility to these types of services and benefits. Typical non-routine decisions are based upon a process in which broadly categorized data may be relevant and need to be considered. In this process, one looks for signs, trends, syndromes, clues, etc., which upon further review of the data would be shown as to whether or not they have substance.[1] The extent to which "meaning" is derived from the data may depend as much on the artfulness of the decision makers and the constraints placed upon them as on the nature and extent of the information.

Influences Upon Decisions

Typically, non-routine decisions fall along a continuum that ranges from the clearly eligible to the clearly ineligible. It is the thesis of this discussion that decisions in the middle range, which are more difficult to make, follow identifiable patterns. Under certain conditions an agency will tend to allow benefits or extend services when in doubt, while other conditions lead to the denial of benefits or services to equally eligible applicants. In attempting to identify these sources of influence, it will be convenient to classify them into three categories of factors related to applicants, to decision makers, and to organizations. Obviously, considerable interaction can be expected among the three sets of factors.

Factors Related to Applicants. This is perhaps the most widely studied set of influences on decisions. One of the prominent themes in the literature concerns the socio-economic status of applicants, their levels of education, and their racial and ethnic backgrounds. The reasoning involved is that low socio-economic and educational backgrounds and membership of certain minority groups tend to be associated with greater selectivity among applicants. Varied explanations are given including the ability of such applicants to articulate and present their cases, their unfamiliarity with procedures and difficulty in interacting with bureaucracies, and the complexity of problems they bring to the agencies. Much less research effort has been directed to discerning the reasons than to verifying selectivity with respect to applicants who possess these characteristics. The influence of such extraneous factors upon screening and service decisions has been reported in a variety of treatment settings and programs. Investigators in a major study of mental illness concluded that "latent social factors besides claimed medical criteria are influential in the determination of *who* is treated, *where, how,* and *for how long.*"[2] Similar conclusions were reached in other studies of treatment of mental illness as summarized in the following generalizations about individuals from low socio-economic backgrounds:

> They are less frequently accepted for treatment, stay in treatment for a shorter period of time, tend to be assigned to lower status personnel, and are more likely to receive somatic as opposed to psychotherapeutic treatment. Social class appears to be inversely related to risk of continuous long term hospitalization but this does not imply treatment. There are at least two studies which suggest that once the low socio-economic person gets in treatment he seems to profit as much as those from other classes. But there is a strong possibility that these patients represent a select population to have gotten into treatment in the first place.[3]

Applicants for disability insurance who were from lower socio-economic and educational backgrounds or who had low intellectual levels of functioning (I.Q.) were found to benefit from direct and comprehensive evaluations.[4] The conclusion drawn from that study was that applicants who come from the lower class, and the lower educational and I.Q. levels are ill-equipped to present their conditions and therefore stand to benefit from multi-disciplinary and direct "clinical" evaluations in contrast to "paper" evaluations. The same study shows significant class differential in the availability and adequacy of information from attending physicians for decision purposes. Not only do more people in the higher socio-economic conditions have private physicians—a fact amply demonstrated in the literature—but also more of them seem to obtain more complete reports in support of their claims.

The influence of racial and ethnic characteristics is mentioned in much of the literature, but few studies provide empirical evidence while controlling class differences which constitute a significant confounding factor, especially in populations seeking services and benefits from most public programs. The absence of racial and ethnic designation from many records rules out the possibility of assessing the current influence of these factors. However, earlier reports indicate racial and ethnic differentials in gate-keeping processes in mental hospitals,[5] in the provision and outcome of social services[6] and in child guidance clinics.[7] A "subtle form of client selection" was reported in the latter clinics:

> Here clients are often accepted in terms of their 'receptivity' to therapy. However, this criterion favors those persons who have been socialized into the middle-class value orientation held by, for example, the clinic staff and the social groups who pay the bill. The poor, especially the families from ethnic groups within the lower class, who according to the ideal norms of these agencies should receive the greatest amount of attention, are quietly shunted aside.[8]

Findings about other programs "show a clear bias in work for the blind in favor of children and employable adults and against elderly blind persons."[9] As will be elaborated later, service organizations tend to favor applicants who possess characteristics that aid the attainment of certain organizational goals.

Stereotyping of certain impairments may have a bearing on decisions concerning benefits. Persons with coronary heart disease were found in one study to be allowed disability benefits more often than those whose chief complaints were low back disorders.[10] These differences persisted in all comparisons while controlling over the degree of severity of physical limitation resulting from the impairments and the prognosis for the conditions. The two types of disorders can be contrasted in many ways. The important characteristic here is that low back disorders have often been linked with psychosomatic problems and at times with malingering.[11] In fact, due to this conception or misconception, a number of rehabilitation facilities do not admit persons with these disorders.[12]

Another theme in the literature concerning applicants' characteristics and their influence on gate-keeping decisions relates to the applicants' persistence in pursuing their claims and the use of advocates and supporters. Almond and Lasswell reported aggressive and persistent behavior on the part of clients of a public insurance agency was characteristic of clients who had been in longer contact with the organization, or who had been employed by government.[13] More of the aggressive clients, compared to the non-aggressive ones, had broken the law and had had contact with penal institutions; tended to come from higher income and educational groups; and more were native born and raised in urban areas. They were more likely to have occupied positions in which they dealt with people rather than with things.

Very little research has been done on the influence of legal counsel and other forms of representation on decisions concerning services and benefits. An analysis of decision reversals by Social Security hearing examiners in cases of disability benefits show that claimants' chances of attaining favorable decisions were improved when accompanied by a physician or lawyer, and were greatly improved when accompanied by the combination of a physician and a lawyer. Reversals of denial decisions for persons with these three forms of representation were higher than those without representation by 10%, 12%, and 26%, respectively.[14] Several explanations can be offered and would require careful controls in order to specify their relative contributions to these decisions. However, regardless of the processes that underlie the relations between representation and gate-keeping decisions, the fact that such relations exist raises an important policy question about equality in access to representation.

Factors Related to Decision Makers. In decisions based on diffuse or especially ambiguous criteria, the tendency is to place greater reliance upon human judgment, resulting in an increased potential for subjective decisions. Diffuseness of criteria permits not only differences in interpretations but also selectivity in evidence. It is perhaps for this reason that the public expects non-routine decisions to be made by "professionals" who possess specialized knowledge relevant to the agency's services. In fact, involvement in gate-keeping decisions has given impetus to the emergence or development of certain professions. Thus, decisions on admissions to hospitals are expected to be made by physicians, on acceptance for rehabilitation services by rehabilitation counselors, and on welfare benefits and services to families by social workers.

Studies concerning the subjective influences of decision-makers on decisions have concentrated on the relative class positions of professionals and clients, the professional orientations of decision-makers, and their ideologies. On the relative class positions, the thesis advanced is that professionals will tend to accept for services clients who resemble them in socio-economic backgrounds and values, and with whom it is easier to communicate.[15] Differences in professional orientations were studied most often among psychiatrists for whom variations in decisions about patients are explained in terms of differences in clinical approaches.[16] Common to such studies is the hypothesis that organically-oriented psychiatrists tend to classify people as psychotics to whom organic treatment are most applicable, while the tendency among psychiatrists with psycho-analytic orientations is to diagnose conditions more often in terms of neurosis to which their clinical approaches would be better suited. Ideologies and other factors have not received empirical attention. Available evidence indicates that characteristics such as liberalism-conservatism, and attitudes toward work ethics influence decisions, especially in regard to allowance and denial of financial assistance and benefits.[17] Also, the length of time decision-makers have been employed in agencies where criteria undergo rapid change seems to be associated with differences in gate-keeping decisions. In some agencies studied by this writer, there was a fast trend toward the liberalization of criteria—that is, to make them less restrictive. Information obtained through these studies shows that decision-makers who have been in the agency for a long period of time tended to be "denial prone" because of being accustomed to the earlier criteria. Newer decision-makers became familiar with only the liberalized criteria and therefore tended to conform to them more closely. Systematic data on the subjective influences of decision-makers remain badly lacking.

Factors Related to Organizations. Organizations develop informal, but nevertheless powerful, norms that come to be shared by those involved in screening decisions. As pointed out earlier, each of these decisions generally entails the risk of committing one of two types of errors; the rejection of a deserving applicant or the acceptance of a non-deserving one.

The norms in question act as social pressures to channel decisions on ambiguous cases into one direction or the other by indicating the type of error more likely to be tolerated. The question then is: What organizational factors lead to a greater tendency to reject or to accept ambiguous cases? Explanations may be simple and perhaps self-evident, but their cumulative effects upon services and the public's reactions are profound.

In identifying some of the important organizational influences on screening decisions we will proceed with stating a series of propositions and the rationale for each including available empirical evidence.

To borrow the market concepts in analyzing the influence of supply and demand for services, it can be said that:

When the balance of services' supply and demand is in favor of supply, the tendency will be to accept doubtful applicants.

The dependence of service agencies on clientele is no less real than that of firms on customers.[18] "Clienteles are not only the initial justification for the creation of an organization, their constant approbation serves as a living sanction for its continuance." Service organizations, especially those of a public nature, are non-profit making. To maintain or increase their resources, they must demonstrate that their services are needed. When the demand for services is low compared to their supply, an organization suffers an "embarrassment of riches" which is perhaps more tolerable to newly established organizations than to others of long standing. In adapting to relatively low demand, service organizations may not only accept dubious clients but may also formally redefine eligibility requirements for services and benefits. Some organizations, as in the case of many public health clinics, actively recruit through various devices that attract new clients and encourage existent ones to maintain their relations to the clinics. Other responses to a shortage in clientele can be seen in the submission of controls over servces as in adult education programs which become dominated by the desires of clients, irrespective of professional standards;[19] and in the tendency to "lock in clients," especially those with characteristics that reflect well on the organization or aid in the attainment of its goals as in certain services for the blind.[20] When the demands for services so decline as to threaten survival, organizations may change their objectives and incorporate others to ensure a new clientele in their scope of services. The history of the National Foundation for Infantile Paralysis is a case in point.[21] With the advent of control over polio, the Foundation changed its title to refer to the disabled in general, and altered its functions in a way that provides for its continuity. Changes in tuberculosis societies and their adoption of other respiratory diseases constitute another example.

> When the balances of services' supply and demand is in favor of demand, the tendency will be to reject doubtful applicants.

No service organization is endowed with unlimited re-sources, and a disproportionate demand for services can strain the resources and require certain adaptations. These strains may cause organizations not only to become informally more selective in the cases of doubtful applicants, but also to make their formal criteria of eligibility more stringent. Some orga-nizations react like traditional economic enterprises and increase the charge assessed clients for services, as in raising the deductible amounts in services under the medicare programs. Others may impose non-pecuniary costs as in waiting time spent in clinics or on waiting lists, or in the form of means-tests administered to applicants for public assistance. Some service organizations have little or no control over the number of admissions. Since these agencies cannot manipulate demand, they adapt to strains in resources primarily by manipulating the supply of services. While in some instances the level of services is lowered for all clients, in others there develops a segregation of clients into sectors to whom differing levels of services are applied. The development of "dumping grounds" in public schools, and the "back wards" in mental hospitals and institutions for the mentally retarded are concrete examples of this process.[22] These comprise persons who are defined as less educable or having severe and difficult problems, and they are relegated to what amounts to merely custodial attention.

An important factor in the balance of supply and demand is the elasticity of the supply of different service elements. Beyond funding, the supply of services depends largely on the elasticity of the supply of facilities, equipment, and personnel.

The first two are generally much more elastic than personnel; that is, their supply responds more quickly to the availability of funds. Increases in the supply of personnel, especially those who require long periods of professional training, is much slower. The shortage of manpower in many service fields is a much discussed issue especially in medicine.[23] It is true that the availability of funds in a given organization may quickly enhance its competitive position for personnel. However, the same cannot be said for manpower on a national level. In other words, while an increase in personnel budget of an organization enables it to attract personnel from other organizations, this type of mobility does not affect the national supply of professionals. We have seen the effects of this inelasticity during the last decade when large amounts of money were funneled into health care programs without a corresponding increase in the supply of trained personnel. The result of the imbalance was that health care became one of the leading sectors of the economy in inflation.

It has already been mentioned that monetary and other costs assessed clients for the services they receive constitute a mechanism by which organizations attempt to lower the levels of demand. Also, costs incurred by organizations in services and benefits can be expected to affect the supply of services, and consequently, the gate-keeping norms. Evidence in support of this proposition can be seen by comparing the stringency of screening processes in two organizations of disability insurance. The cost of a claim for benefits allowed under the federal program is many times that allowed under the temporary disability insurance programs maintained by some states. A much more elaborate procedure is followed in the first program in establishing the legitimacy of a claim, while most of the latter programs simply depend on reports from attending physicians. It is true that careful scrutiny in processing applications for costly claims and services also enhances accuracy and thereby protects the rights of applicants. However, evidence suggests a greater tendency in such programs toward rejection than acceptance of doubtful cases.[24]

The range of utility of a service can also be expected to affect the demand for it. Some organizations are engaged in income maintenance through insurance, compensation, and public assistance payments; others provide food stamps, clothing, and similar commodities; still others offer such highly personal services as chest x-rays and other health-related tests. The range of utility of these services decreases as we move from the first to the last. Money is easier to exchange than commodities, and personalized services like preventive health tests and examinations are useful only to the individuals on whom they are performed. The range of utility of a service determines the choices a recipient can make. Since a wider range of choices is more appealing it can be hypothesized that the greater the range of utility of a service, the higher the demand for it.

Another factor that relates to the demand for services is the degree to which stigma is attached to their recipients. For example, applicants for public assistance are believed to be more stigmatized than applicants for workmen's compensation or disability and sickness insurance benefits. Also, greater stigmatization is attached to mental disorders and venereal diseases than to other types of organic conditions. Stigma and associated social pressures can be expected to exert significant inhibiting influences on demand for services.

Economic mechanisms by themselves cannot fully explain variations in supply and demand for services. In the *ideal* form of free market economy, price originates in the market and serves to regulate supply and demand. Higher prices result in lowered demand and increased supply, and vice versa. For a variety of reasons that need not be elaborated here, this ideal form of economic exchange is nowhere practiced on an appreciable scale, especially in the allocation of resources for services and their distributions.[25] Societies do not attach a market value to such services as education, health care, and welfare, nor do organizations assess recipients the full cost of the services they receive. Expenditures are certainly considered in decisions to initiate and expand services, but by no means are the only factor. The history of service legislation is replete with expensive programs that were enacted, and with others defeated in spite of the relatively modest costs. Pressures for the allocation of resources, which determine the supply of services, are generated through the political processes by which individuals and groups articulate interests and make demands upon the political decision makers.[26] Of particular relevance is the role played by the service agencies and organizations themselves in promoting interests and affecting decisions concerning increases in the supply of their services. They attempt to document the existence of needs for the services they offer, to demonstrate effectiveness in meeting their goals, and to gain public support for these goals. At times, these attempts influence gate-keeping decisions in directions inconsistent with the clients' interests.

The more quantifiable the indicators of service effectiveness, the greater the tendency to reject applicants when in doubt.

Criteria for service effectiveness may be more or less quantifiable. To illustrate, the results of employment or vocational rehabilitation services are more quantifiable than those of public health clinics. The first two types of services are aimed at persons who are unemployed because of the labor market or because of a disability. Effectiveness consists of placing a client in a job—an identifiable and measurable outcome. Differential rates of successful rehabilitation and work placement thus provide the basis for quantitative, and less disputable, assessments of the effectiveness of organizations and personnel. In contrast, it would be difficult to identify quantitative results that can be attributed, for example, to a maternal and child health clinic or a family planning clinic, or to particular members of their staffs. Because it is difficult to evaluate the effectiveness of organizations or personnel in these types of services, their reports usually emphasize activities rather than results. Such reports are typically organized around miles traveled, meetings attended, and numbers of people contacted.

When service results are relatively quantifiable, a premium is placed on "successful case closures." This criterion becomes incorporated in the organization's reward system, and fosters an avoidance of risks in applicants accepted for services. The question is whether clients who represent minimal risks actually need the services or are included primarily for boosting the numbers of "successful closures." A form of specialization may develop in some organizations, in attempting to cope with problems of selectivity, by assigning certain personnel to the more difficult cases.

The quantifiability of results may also lead to goal displacement when "success" in achieving the emergent goals is more easily measurable than the organization's original goals. In sheltered workshops, for instance, economic returns for the organizations in many cases have subverted the original goals of serving the disabled. While the idea is to help the disabled find their way to competitive employment, sheltered workshops often retain the better workers because of the greater economic contributions they make to the organizations. Another form of goal displacement was reported in some agencies where efficiency in case processing, which is a quantifiable goal, displaced or competed with the agencies' stated service goals.[27]

The probability of a doubtful applicant being accepted or rejected by a given service organization relates to differences in referring organizations.

Organizations seek from each other whatever they need in pursuing their own objectives.[28] One of these lacks, of course, can be clients through whose presence organizations document the needs for their services. When demand is low relative to the supply of services, an organization responds more readily to others from which it receives many referrals, and dubious cases referred by such organizations have a greater chance of being accepted. The receiving agency may also extend some of its other resources to the appropriate organizations in exchange for a continuation or increase in the number of referrals. On the other hand, when demand is greater than supply, referrals would probably be accepted more readily from organizations that are also contributing other resources. Other than clients, contributions of one organization to another may be in the form of facilities, funds, personnel, services, or support in affecting favorable political decisions. When members of an organization can decide on the resources of another organization and how they are to be used, they can exercise certain influence by virtue of this position. The problem is illustrated by Schwartz who points out that in the case of some public services agencies "a discharge of their adjudicatory function in a truly judicial manner is rendered somewhat difficult by the frequent intervention by individual congressmen in claims in which they are interested."[29]

When the services of an organization are controversial, gate-keeping decisions will be influenced less by organizational norms and more by the orientations of individual decision makers.

Organizational goals vary in the degree of public acceptance and support. Education and health care generally enjoy relatively greater concensus when compared to the considerable controversy that surrounds such welfare and insurance programs as public assistance, aid for dependent children, and disability insurance. Organizations administering controversial services are caught in a "double bind" in measuring the fulfillment of their goals. The most concrete indicators, similar to the number of students and the costs of education, are the numbers of beneficiaries and the amounts of funds provided. However, unlike the measures of education, controversial benefits are challenged as either too large or too small. On the one hand, with many recipients receiving a large total of benefits, the question is whether public funds are being used to perpetuate dependency. On the other hand, if the number of recipients and amounts of benefits are small, the public may denounce the screening criteria as too stringent to satisfy the goals of the program. No clear norms for gate-keeping decisions can be expected under such conditions, for both sides of the argument about goals are likely to pervade the organization itself. The most likely delineation of positions within these organizations is the professional and bureaucratic orientations: "the professional is bound by a norm of service and code of ethics to represent the welfare and interests of his clients, whereas the bureaucrat's foremost responsibility is to represent and promote the interests of his organization."[30]

In the absence of generally accepted organizational norms, the biases of individual decision-makers may assume greater significance in the screening of doubtful cases. When services are controversial, organizations can also be expected to place greater emphasis upon objectivity and specificity of criteria. For such organizations, criteria for acceptance or rejection of applicants become as much an element in the controversy as the services themselves.

The actions of organizations are not only oriented toward goal attainment and adaptation to the external environment, but also toward the maintenance of internal integration.[31] The patterns of interaction between organizations and clients vary in the degree of threat they pose to the authority structure of the organizations and to the morale of the staffs. This is particularly the case in facilities dealing with long term therapies and services. It is no accident that many such facilities resist the concept of therapeutic communities where patients assume active roles in connection with services and other aspects of their institutional life. Related to this point is the distinction between "inducting organizations" in which "the client becomes a client-member," and other service organizations where clients "remain outside the boundary of the organization's authority structure."[32] For example, residents in a hospital or students in a graduate program who are also engaged in teaching differ in many respects from patients in an out-patient clinic or recipients of welfare benefits. Not all inducting organizations require the same degree of involvement from client -members, nor are all inducting organizations equally specific in their interaction with clients.[33] However, because interaction between client-members and the professional staffs of inducting organizations is more intense and because client members generally influence the organization more than the other types of clients, it can be expected that inducting organizations would tend to be more selective in gate-keeping decisions than other service organizations. The foregoing discussion leads to a proposition that can be stated at a more abstract level as follows:

The more diffuse the interaction between clients and service organizations, the greater the tendency to reject applicants when in doubt.

These propositions stating relationships between organizational attributes and gate-keeping decisions by no means constitute an exhaustive list, nor do they all represent verified generalizations. The puropose is merely to illustrate the potential influences upon gate-keeping decisions in organizations dealing with benefits and services when clear and demonstrable norms of validity are lacking.

Implications of Gate-Keeping Decisions

Gate-keeping decisions represent a crucial link in applicants' encounters with service organizations and professions. Over the years, these decisions have contributed to the erosion of confidence and trust on the part of clients and the public at large, and to role strains among professionals. The pursuit of organizational and professional objectives is resented when inconsistent with clients' interests or accorded priority over optimal provision of services. Several manifestations of the use of gate-keeping decisions in such pursuits have become widely shared knowledge.

The *first* of these manifestations arises in connection with the attempts of service organizations to legitimize their existence or justify an expansion in their services or domains. The process is usually one of documenting unmet demands for services—a process than entails direct or indirect solicitation of applicants. Although unfulfilled demands constitute convincing evidence of the need for greater resources, failure to meet such demands can be a source of much frustration especially for applicants encouraged by the organizations themselves.

Secondly, as pointed out, in the early stages organizations may lack clients and therefore are less selective in their gate-keeping operations. As clientele builds up, these organizations apply more stringent criteria and become less accepting of doubtful cases. These shifts add to the frustration and confusion of clients.

Thirdly, negative attitudes are also likely to form on the part of related public when organizations restrict services to applicants who represent minimal risks of "failure." It has already been mentioned that this tendency is characteristic of organizations with the more quantifiable criteria for assessing the outcome of services. For a service organization to ignore applicants with severe problems is contrary to expectations based on the notion that the greater the problem the greater the need for services.

Fourthly, for some applicants, specialization compounds the effects of gate-keeping decisions of service agencies. Specialization is an inevitable outcome of the phenomenal growth in knowledge and techniques. And, although functional in many respects, specialization has resulted in dysfunctional fragmentation of many programs. Because of the tendency of organizations to avoid overlap in domains, as new programs are introduced a consequent differentiation of functions takes place among agencies where the boundaries of existent ones are re-examined and criteria of eligibility are reset.[34] This is particularly true of public services perhaps with the possible exception of OEO programs. This process of differentiation of organizational boundaries seems to affect some of the applicants with the greatest need but also with the greatest difficulty in qualifying for public programs, because any single limitation is not severe enough to make them eligible for services or benefits under a particular program. Though so marginal to all criteria as to be excluded from each single program, in sum they suffer from a greater overall limitation than those defined as eligible. Among applicants for disability benefits, for example, some were denied benefits because their disability was "not severe enough," and yet were also rejected by rehabilitation agencies because their disability was "too severe to be rehabilitated."[35]

A *fifth* and subtle effect of organizational gate-keeping processes is that of role strain among professionals. Members of the professions participate in the gate-keeping decisions of service organizations in one or a combination of three ways: (a) as members of the staffs of organizations, (b) as consultants in the evaluation of applicants, but paid by the organizations, and (c) as attending clinicians who submit reports on behalf of their patients or clients. In these roles, professionals either make the decisions themselves or help shape them through information they provide. Role strains arise in situations where professionals encounter pressures to render information or judgments, or to act in ways inconsistent with their conceptions of professional norms. Such pressures may come from organizations, clients, or from wider segments of the public. To begin with, incompatibilities between gate-keeping and therapeutic functions constitute a general source of strain. The screening of applicants is in effect a certification for the services or benefits they seek, and implies policing of the boundaries of service organizations. The involvement of professionals in these functions structures their relationships to clients in a way that is incompatible with requisites for effectiveness in therapy or other forms of help.

It has already been mentioned that gate-keeping decisions are often used by organizations in adjusting to their environmental pressures. A second source of role strain results from the transfer of these pressures to decision making professionals in the form of constraints on their decisions. Thus, some professionals find themselves screening out applicants who, in the professional's judgment, are more deserving of the services. This problem is more characteristic of organizations in which performance criteria are quantifiable than those with non-measurable outcomes. In the former types of organizations, as pointed out earlier, the tendency is toward greater selectivity in admissions favoring those who are more likely to show successful conclusions of services. This type of role strain was reported among rehabilitation counselors:

> . . . strain in the counselor's role is caused by the *materialistic orientation of the role*, which is 'product' oriented (placement as employed) rather than humanistically oriented (the sicker they are, the more services they should get). The reason this is a strain to the counselor is due to the normal definition of the counseling role as a 'helping' role, and the expectations of the disabled in this regard.[36]

A third example of role strain stems from pressures upon professionals to submit reports favoring their clients' applications for benefits or services.[37] The pressure here takes the form of fear of losing clients. Client choices constitute a form of control in that "they determine the survival of a profession or a specialty, as well as the career success of particular professionals." When asked to certify the eligibility of a client or patient for a service or benefit, the clinician has limited alternatives. He can write and document the case for his client. This alternative poses no problem if the clinician actually believes the client qualifies for the services or benefits he is seeking. However, if the professional believes the client is not qualified, any of the available alternatives would entail some strain. He may refuse to cooperate, or may send information detrimental to this patient's claim; in either case he would be risking the loss of a client. Another alternative would be to document the case for his client, a situation that entails a violation of professional standards and norms.

The structure of gate-keeping decisions poses a special dilemma to institutions whose operations are organized around interprofessional teamwork. This century has witnessed a remarkable increase in the numbers of new service professions and in the degree of specialization within the established ones. Greater specialization and proliferation of professions inevitably calls for coordination. One approach to coordination that has become prevalent in many contemporary forms of service delivery systems is that of teamwork. Combinations of psychiatrists, psychologists, social workers, occupational therapists, physical therapists, nurses, vocational counselors, pediatricians, and members of other specialties and professions constitute teams in a variety of pediatric, psychiatric, rehabilitation, and other service settings. Cooperation among members of the teams is an essential element to their effectiveness. One study concluded that:

> Cooperation among professional persons is at once the easiest and most difficult of relationships to achieve.
>
> It is the easiest because service to others is always a part of the standards of professional bodies, and members place great value upon these standards. Because of this fact it is easy for persons from different professions to join hands in a shared purpose.
>
> It is most difficult because in order to have true cooperation there must be trust and understanding among those who would work together. The members of various professions bring their own points of view, social positions, and skills to the collaborative relation. These differences may hinder the development of confidence and mutual agreement.[38]

Differences among professions in points of view, skills, and social positions are as manifested in gate-keeping decisions as in any other aspect of the services. Team approaches are based upon the assumption that clients' problems are complex and involve facets that can be better understood and ameliorated through specialized knowledge and skills possessed by different professions. Two patterns of decision making have evolved, each entailing a major limitation. The *first* pattern is to assign gate-keeping decisions to the representatives of a given profession who become "coordinators." Gate-keeping decisions here may extend beyond the admission and rejection of applicants, to referral to other professionals for services. Consequently, these coordinators are in effect gate-keepers in relation to the other professions represented on the team. Members of the other professions are brought into contact with the client when the coordinator detects a problem that requires the services of these professions. The limitation inherent in this model lies in the ability of a person with a given professional background to recognize problems that fall in the domains of other professions. To illustrate, can a social worker make a differential diagnosis of physical conditions? Or can a nurse take the place of a psychologist or a social worker in identifying emotional and social problems? Aside from these technical considerations, gate-keeping power structures the relationships among members of clinical and other service teams in a way that fosters resentments on the part of many.

The *second* pattern of decision making in interprofessional teams grants greater recognition to specialization and appeals more to democratic principles. Representatives of each profession on the team are given the opportunity to contact the client and determine the presence or absence of problems within their domains. The limitation of this approach is that it works more for the convenience and interests of the professionals than the clients. To demonstrate their importance to the teams, professionals may tend to overdiagnose problems among clients.

Alternatives To Validity

The foregoing discussion leads to a number of conclusions. To begin with, the reasons for which service organizations and professions are initiated are not necessarily the ones that nurture their survival and growth. Organizational and professional interests assume independent significance and become ends in themselves. The pursuit of these interests often gains priority over concern with services to clients even when conflicting with clients' interests.

It can be concluded also that gate-keeping decisions constitute a point of leverage which service organizations and professions use in the pursuit of their interests. Such decisions become more manipulatible when they are of a non-routine nature. As pointed out earlier, non-routine decisions are generally placed in the hands of professionals who presumably possess specialized knowledge and skills relevant to the problems in question. Entrusting gate-keeping decisions to professionals is predicated upon the assumption that relevant knowledge and skills mean an independent and objective application of norms and criteria of validity. However, there is paradox involved here in the sense that the openness of non-routine decisions to the exercise of judgment indicates incomplete and non-specifiable knowledge concerning the problems—that is ambiguity in the norms and criteria of validity.

A third conclusion is that there has been an increasing awareness of the vast imbalance in power when organizations are compared to individuals. This imbalance is even greater in regard to individuals in need of services and resources controlled by given organizations. While the decisions of organizations can drastically effect the welfare and at times the very survival of an applicant for services, the decisions of typical individual applicants would have little if any influence on organizations.

It is within the context of these three conclusions, and particularly the absence of shared and demonstrable norms of validity for decisions on services and benefits, that the search for alternatives can be understood. Attempts in that direction generally revolve around the norms of *justice* and *equity*.

On the part of some organizations there have been sustained efforts toward further specification of eligibility criteria in order to move the decision making process toward the routine end of the continuum. Often pressures for specification of meaning and exactness of criteria lead to "premature closure."[39] There is no physiological or other reason for age 65 to be more appropriate for receiving retirement benefits than 64 or 66. Nor is there any reason to suppose that age is the only or even the most valid indicator in the interest of society or the individual. Other examples of simple clear-cut criteria being used for decisions on complex phenomena can be seen in the use of age also as a criterion for admission to public schools, and the use of "impairment schedules" for the purpose of compensating work-related injuries and impairments. The appeal of exact and objective criteria in program operations is that they simplify the structure of decision-making and enhance the reliability of decisions by reducing random errors. And, some sense of "justice" derives from uniformity in the application of criteria even when arbitrary and entailing systematic errors.

Some organizations approach the norms of justice directly through what students of jurisprudence call "reasoned decisions," that is, by requiring a written rationale for decisions reached. Among other objectives, this requirement has the effect of evoking care in the reasoning process on the part of decision makers. Few organizations employ a decision-making structure that adheres to the "due process," the basic elements of which are to be heard orally; present evidence and argument; rebut adverse evidence, through cross-examination and other appropriate means; have the decision based only upon known evidence; and appear with counsel.[40] The complexity of such decision-making processes and the costs of legal and other forms of representation favor applicants and claimants from the higher levels of education and socio-economic backgrounds.[41]

Clear symptoms of client alienation and rebellion, and challenges to the traditional view that the primary commitments of members of the service professions are to the welfare clients, have brought about several movements toward balancing the power of organizations and enhancing possibilities of recourse for applicants denied services and benefits. Among these movements is one toward the employment of indigenous groups to man the boundaries of service organizations in their interaction with applicants and clients. The principle is to enhance communication, however, the practice also creates greater balance between organizations and clients at these junctures of interaction.

The spread of "ombudsmen" in hasty and faddish ways constitutes another form of response. The idea here is to provide a neutral corner where disputes can be attended and some action be persuaded. The establishment of the Administrative Conference of the U.S. with the mandate to study the administrative operations of the government and to report to the agencies, to the President, and to Congress about needed change, is also a step in that direction. The emphasis on consumer education which is becoming a major concern in research and development in health services and other types of human services are oriented to preparing citizens for recognizing and pursuing their rights to these services.

Distrustful of service organizations and professions, clients and related publics are seeking other means to bring their own interests directly to those who allocate resources. The popularity of consumer advocates, the formation of welfare rights organizations, the marches of the poor on Washington and other forms of advocacy are manifestations of this process. A recent legislation establishing a national Office of Child Advocacy implies a recognition of a need once considered as being met by services, organizations and professions.

Most of the attempts described above are unsystematic and feeble. Many of them have served more as pacifiers than as serious steps toward change. Perhaps one important reason is the absence of clear direction for change in the form of future models for service organizations. To be useful, such models would need to minimize the problems identified; to build into the reward system reinforcement for an orientation and a commitment to optimal services; to afford applicants and clients assistance through the complexity of today's systems of services, and a redress for their grievances. Organizational analysts and planners have not as yet provided such a model.

Relevance To Evaluation

The papers already presented and the discussions they generated have thoughtfully and skillfully addressed several aspects of evaluation; primarily methodology, models, roles of evaluators, and the contexts of evaluation. In this paper I chose to concentrate on a substantive theme with the hopes of conveying a number of important points concerning evaluation. To begin with, in evaluation as in other types of research, the problem ought to determine the methodological approaches, and the designs and requirements for evaluating outcome differ from those appropriate for evaluating aspects of the process.

Emphasis has been primarily placed on obtaining valid measures of outcome in the sense of change in clients and their conditions consistent with the service objectives of programs being evaluated. It is proposed in this paper that equal attention be given to developing ways to assess processes and outcomes according to standards and norms of justice and equity. This, of course, calls for the inclusion of information about the opinions of applicants, clients, and other members of the public in the data systems being used in policy formulations and program operations.

Another message intended in this presentation is that much of the current evaluation research is sterile in the sense that neither offers explanations nor directions for change. Time pressures and inappropriate patterns of funding have combined to produce evaluations that are conceptually pedestrian and methodologically faulty. The only purpose such work might serve is perhaps to reinforce biases and prejudices, and to justify decisions already reached. For sound policy and program analysis, four types of data are necessary: (a) information directly from applicants, clients, and other segments of the public; (b) information from providers of services and administrators in service programs expressing their individual opinions; (c) official reports of agencies; and (d) comparative data on similar programs and agencies in other societies, especially comparable ones. The flow of such information would need to be planned on a longitudinal basis in order to afford the opportunity to examine change and the factors that contribute to it. In short, the value of evaluative data can be immensely improved if provided within explanatory and predictive frameworks.

A final point to be made concerns the often mentioned dilemma inherent in the role of evaluators. Those who see a dilemma describe it at least in part as follows: To gain sufficient knowledge about a program a researcher will need to become heavily involved in the program and therefore would stand to develop commitment to it and lose objectivity. Lack of knowledge is certainly more equitable with ignorance than with loss of objectivity. There are no data to prove this, but I would hypothesize that more faulty research and evaluation has resulted from ignorance on the part of investigators than from bias toward certain findings. As has been pointed out by others: one should not enter evaluative or other research with an empty mind, but hopefully with an open one. With great appreciation for the role of serendipity, it is still imperative that evaluators and researchers possess depth knowledge about the programs they are to evaluate. Studies whether or not of an evaluative nature are actually verificational vehicles for ideas investigators must have beforehand. It is equally important that investigators be insulated against pressures and constraints that might conceivably affect their performance.

While ideal states are often difficult to identify, let alone attain, it is possible to approximate conditions necessary for effective evaluations.

Footnotes for Chapter 3

[1] J. B. Stone, "A Diagrammatic Conceptual System for Interpreting Assessment Data," A paper presented at the N.I.M.H.-Peace Corps Conference, Washington, D.C., March, 1963.

[2] A. B. Hollingshead and F. C. Redlich, Social Class and Mental Illness, (New York: John Wiley and Sons, 1958).See also Srole, L., et al., Mental Health in the Metropolis, The Midtown Manhattan Study. New York: McGraw-Hill Book Company, 1965; and "The Differential Use and Outcome of Children's Psychiatric Clinic Service, "Smith College Studies in Social Work, Vol. 25, No. 2 (February 1955), pp. 1-10.

[3] K. S. Miller and C. M. Grigg, Mental Health and the Lower Social Classes (Tallahassee: The Florida State University, 1966), pp. 55–56.

[4] S. Z. Nagi, Disability and Rehabilitation: Legal, Clinical, and Self-Concepts and Measurement (Columbus, Ohio: The Ohio State University Press, 1969).

[5] See for example J. See, Insanity Proceedings and the p,atterning of Black-White State Hospital Admission Rate Differentials (Blacksburg, Virginia: Virginia Polytechnic Institute, 1971).

[6] See for example A. Garcia, "The Chicano and Social Work," *Social Casework, Vol. 52, 1971, pp. 274-78; Turner, F., "Ethnic Differences and Client Performance,"* Social Service Review, Vol. 44, March 1970, pp. 1-10; and Welfare Grants Divisions, Canadian Department of National Health and Welfare, *Ethnic Factors in the Provision and Outcome of Social Work Services,* Report on project 555/25/1, Ottawa, 1971.

[7] G. Sjoberg, et al., "Bureaucracy and the Lower Class." *Sociology and Social Research,* Vol. 50 (April, 1966), pp. 325-337.

[8] *Ibid.*

[9] R. A. Scott, "The Selection of Clients by Social Welfare Agencies: The Case of the Blind." *Social Problems,* Vol. 14 (Winter 1967), pp. 248-257.

[10] S. Z. Nagi, *op. cit.*

[11] For example, See E. Weiss, and O. E. English, *Psychosomatic Medicine,* New York: W. B. Sanders, 1957, pp. 112; and Kessler, H. H.; *Low Back Pain in Industry,* New York: Commerce and Industrial Association, 1955.

[12] See *Directory of Institutional Members,*(Evanston, Illinois: Association of Rehabilitation Centers, Inc., 1962). The reports of a number of facilities during the period covered exclude "back cases."

[13] Almond and Lasswell, quoted in Blau P. and W. Scott, *Formal Organizations: A Comparative Approach* (San Francisico: Chandler Publishing Co., 1962), pp. 81-82.

[14] For example see M. Rock, "An Evaluation of the SSA Appeals Process," Social Security Administration, Operations Research Staff, Progress Reports 1967-1969.

[15] D. Fanshel, "A Study of Caseworkers' Perceptions of Their Clients," *Social Casework,* Vol. 39, 1958, pp. 543-551.

[16] See A. B. Hollingshead, and F. C. Redlich, *op. cit.*; Raines, G. A., and J. N. Rohmen, "The Operational Matrix of Psychiatric I: Consistency and Variability in Interview Impressions of Different Psychiatrists," *American Journal of Psychiatry,* III, Vol. 10 (April 1955), pp. 721-733.

[17] Unpublished material resulting from the writer's research.

[18] W. J. Gore and J. W. Dyson (eds.) *The Making of Decisions.* New York: The Free Press, 1964.

[19] See for example R. Petersen and W. Petersen, *University Adult Education: A Guide to Policy* (New York: Harper and Row, 1960); and Clark, B. R., *Adult Education in Transition.* (Berkeley: University of California Press, 1956).

[20] R. A. Scott, "The Factory as a Social Service Organization: Goal Displacement in Workshops for the Blind." *Social Problems,* Vol. 15, No. 2 (Fall 1967), pp. 160-175.

[21] D. L. Sills, *The Volunteers* (Glencoe, Illinois: The Free Press, 1957).

[22] R. O. Carlson, "Environmental Constraints and Organizational Consequences: The Public School and Its Clients." In D. E. Griffiths (ed.) *Behavorial Science and Educational Administration Yearbook.* Chicago: National Society for the Study of Education, 1964.

[23] See for example H. Somers, and A. Somers, *Doctors, Patients, and Health Insurance* (Washington, D. C.: The Brookings Institution, 1961); Kissick W.,

"Health Manpower in Transition," *Milbank Memorial Fund Quarterly*, Vol. XLVI (January 1968), pp. 53-90.

[24] The denial rates of claims for disability insurance benefits under social security are greater than three times as large as for claims for temporary disability insurance benefits.

[25] For further discussion, see T. A. Marschack, "Economic Theories of Organization." In J. G. March (ed.) *Handbook of Organizations.* (Chicago: Rand McNally and Company, 1965).

[26] G. A. Almond and G. B. Powell, *Comparative Politics: A Development Approach* (Boston: Little Brown, 1966).

[27] P. M. Blau, *The Dynamics of Bureaucracy* (Chicago: University of Chicago Press, 1955).

[28] S. Levine and P. E. White, "Exchange as a Conceptual Framework for the Study of Inter-organizational Relationships." *Administrative Science Quarterly*, Vol. 5, 1961, pp. 583-601.

[29] B. Schwartz, *An Introduction to American Administrative Law.* (London: Sir Isaac Pitman and Sons, Ltd., 1962).

[30] P. M. Blau, and W. R. Scott, *Formal Organizations: A Comparative Approach* (San Francisco: Chandler Publishing Company, 1962).

[31] T. Parsons, "An Outline of the social System," in Parsons, T,, Shills, E.' Naegele, C.; and Pits, J. (eds.) Theories of Society (Glencoe, Illinois: The Free Press 1961), pp. 30-79.

[32] C. E. Bidwell, and R. S. Vreeland, "College Education and Moral Orientations: An Organizational Approach." *Administrative Science Quarterly*, Vol. 8 (September 1963), pp. 166-191.

[33] *Ibid.*

[34] S. Levine, and P. White, *op. cit.*

[35] S. Z. Nagi, *op. cit.*

[36] E. A. Krause, "Structured Strain in a Marginal Profession: Rehabilitation Counselling." *Journal of Health and Social Behavior*, Vol. 6, No. 1, 1965, pp. 55-62.

[37] Mark Field, "Structural Strain in the Role of the Soviet Physician," *American Journal of Sociology*, Vol. IVIII, 1953, pp. 493-502.

[38] A. Zander. A. Cohen, and E. Stotland, *Role Relation in the Mental Health Professions.*(Ann Arbor:University of Michigan, Institute for Social Research), 1957.

[39] For further discussion, see A. Kaplan, *The Conduct of Inquiry,* (San Francisco: Chandler Publishing Company, 1964).

[40] B. Schwartz, *op. cit.*

[41] See S. Z. Nagi, *op. cit.* and Rock, M. *op. cit.*

COMMENTARY

John H. Behling

After careful review I found Dr. Nagi's paper both intellectually exciting and stimulating. These observations have led me not so much to a criticism of specific points in his paper but rather it has aroused by own thinking and concern for the involvement of client-consumers in service organizations. I am particularly concerned with the phenomenon so carefully examined by Dr. Nagi of organizational pre-selection and exclusion of clients which places considerable restraints on client involvement and participation in social service agency decision-making.

Who Should Measure Phenomena?

For anything to be measured, someone must be aware and/ or highly conscious of a phenomenon. If we are interested in observing and measuring an event, a social concern, opinion, attitude or feeling, then it must be observed by someone. In times past the expert (an authority figure) observed the behavior (phenomenon) of others and determined (measured) the nature (definition) of the phenomenon. This view of the role of the expert is still prevalent but it is fast passing into disrepute as totalitarian and undemocratic. Another means of measuring phenomena is to have the respondent with a particular behavior we are interested in measuring observe and measure his own behavior and report the nature of that behavior. In actual practice these two approaches represent polarized views, yet most situations require a combination of these two in some kind of cooperative effort. The second approach seems more valid because only the consumer can best judge what is happening to him. After all, the consumer is the experience. W. I. Thomas' phenomenologied view aptly points out in relation to this point that, "A situation defined as real is real in its consequences." Hence, the participant or consumer must be a part of the evaluation process.

Evaluation For Whom

Evaluation research, it seems to me, is almost entirely done to reassure the sponsors of the program being evaluated of what they already know. If this is so, then why should the sponsors even bother to have evaluation research done? It may very well be because the evaluation as an activity provides the financial supports of the sponsor's program with a rational reason to continue doing what they have been doing. There is a certain political motivation to the evaluation process and such motivation almost entirely ignores the content of the evaluation findings by emphasizing the fact that evaluation has or will occur. Creating real political insight within the community is an exceedingly difficult task under the best of circumstances. The fact is that, at best, making the community aware of the presence of evaluation is an important achievement. Therefore, research evaluation is an activity that reassures all of us: sponsors, evaluators, planners, financial supporters, clients, consumers, decision-makers, and the community.

The proposition that evaluation research is done to reassure the program sponsors of what they already know is not necessarily deceptive since the community may and frequently does demand accountability to the public regarding programs that serve the public interest. The very fact that evaluation research is being done is reassuring to the community.

Evaluation As Process

The whole evaluation process clearly effects the phenomenon being evaluated. It affects the people involved with the phenomenon being evaluated and the numerous processes people are involved with during the evaluation.

Evaluation as a process should be concerned with the processes of program and its measurement and identification of phenomena rather than the so-called "end results." Is anything ever a result of anything or is it merely a part of a subtler process? My conclusion is that it is a process, as are all phenomena. Some phenomena are more often identified by standardized measuring tools used by a known community of qualified professionals. The specific activity observed may be considered a "result" with all the clarity of an absolute. However, this seems to be a function of all measuring tools and the community values at that given time. "Results" seem to be the only observations of an activity and/or process. All phenomena are at varying levels of human consciousness. These phenomena we identify as "results" are simply those entities that are highly visible and awake to the conscious mind of everyone or nearly everyone. Other "results" are present but hardly, perhaps not at all, conscious to anyone. The notion that concrete results exist only to be measured is more often an elusion which in turn is subject to numerous interpretations. After all, what may be a positive "result" today may well become a grossly negative consequence six months from now. On the other hand, "process" is difficult to identify and measure, but it is probably closer to the truth. We can rarely, if at all, observe concrete results in human service programs as single observable entities, but rather are observing relationships between entities. There seems to be no meaning in single identifiable results only in their relationship as part of process.

PART II

THE TECHNOLOGICAL PROBLEMS

CHAPTER 4

Experimental Design in Social Intervention
Programs: Some Perspectives on Evaluation

Louis D. Higgs

Introduction

For the past six months I have been on leave from Ohio State working at the National Science Foundation in one of the most exciting and challenging, yet high risk and frustrating programs in the country. It is a unique program since, in so far as I am aware, along with a parallel program in the National Bureau of Standards, it is the only Federal program established explicitly for systematic social experimentation which is to be conducted by a non-mission agency with no mandate for implementing the results of its experiments. The program is the Experimental R&D Incentives Program and its purpose is to develop policy options for federal activity to stimulate technological innovation and the increased utilization of R&D in the civil sector through the development and conduct of systematic experiments which test various prospective mechanisms. I have been working as a program officer in the Public Sector Office of the Program with primary responsibility for identifying and developing systematic experiments on mechanisms to increase the application of science and technology for the improvement of public services and on ways in which the federal government can incentivize such mechanisms. The program is a policy research program which is aimed not directly at improving such services but rather at learning how to improve them.

When the Symposium invited me to speak several months ago, I was deeply involved in addressing myself to such questions as how much emphasis to place on the initiation of new experiments vis-a-vis the evaluation of "natural experiments" or on-going social interventions and programs. I felt at that time that the obvious substantive differences between the R&D Incentives Program and the variety of human services programs in which you are interested were not as important as the process similarities in trying to develop and evaluate effective public strategies and programs. Thus, I was initially enthusiastic about participating in the Symposium. But, as time passes, the normal panic sets in when one realizes that one is to speak to an audience of experts. Many of you know more about the many technologies subsumed under the rubric of program evaluation than I and many others of you have more experience and insight into the problems and workings of human services programs. I decided that rather than try to go into a detailed discussion of the problems and techniques of experimental evaluation, or a quasi-technical comparison of experimental evaluation and post-hoc evaluation, or a description of the R&D Incentives Program and its relevance to your activities, what I would try to do is share with you in a quite discursive way some of my perspectives on the nature of evaluation and its relation to other forms of human activity and in so doing be sufficiently provocative to stir up some debate.

It is terribly tempting for a non-expert in speaking to experts to do one of two things; either to make the speech, given at every conference or symposium, which points out that the conference or symposium is directed to the wrong questions; or to speed quickly to the meta-questions, i.e., either giving an evaluation or entering into a deep philosophical discussion of the underlying assumptions. The latter is particularly tempting when one believes, as I do, that the basic failures and problems are primarily epistemological issues about which most modern thinking and most practice particularly in the social arena make a number of fundamental mistakes. But rather than enter into a deep philosophical discussion, I would like to make three simple points and touch briefly on their implications, namely:

1.   That evaluation is, in my judgment, part of sound planning, decision-making, and management, is therefore a tool ultimately and thus primarily for action, and is and should be ascientific and inevitably political;
2.   that systematic experimentation or quasi-experimentation has substantial advantages over evaluative analysis relative to improving social services and viewing evaluation through the experimental perspective and the problems of evaluating experiments sheds some useful light on the problems of evaluation and how to cope with them; and finally
3.   that experimentation can be viewed and often conducted as part of an architectural and engineering design process rather than as a quasi-scientific endeavor.

I hope that from the explication of these points, you will come to understand that my paper is quietly heretical, rejecting substantial parts of the conventional wisdom of the new scientism or new rationalism, and that my theme is really deeply philosophical, namely, a call for a more balanced interaction between knowledge and action and a proper understanding of the sequencing of that interaction.

One final prefatory remark. This is not, nor is it meant to be, a scholarly paper. Thus, one will find no footnotes and few references or acknowledgements in the text. I am a firm believer in eclecticism so that a few of the ideas I will present originated with me.*

Evaluation as Policy Research— Knowledge For Action

My first point, namely, that evaluation is a planning, decision-making and management tool whose purpose is to develop knowledge for action seems like a rather placid and common observation unlikely to cause much debate. Yet, If we reflect on it briefly, it may cause more heated debate than we are willing to handle now. For example, note that I say knowledge for action, not into action, and theory for practice, not into practice, because I wanted to indicate the reciprocal relation of knowledge and action. Most of the discussion of policy planning, evaluation, action research, etc., emphasizes only one side of that relationship, namely the degree to which knowledge, analysis, inference processes should guide and direct the action process. It ignores or merely pays lip service to the other side of that relationship, namely, that action does and should structure and guide the process of acquiring and refining knowledge. Here I refer not only to purpose or mission, but also to other factors in the action process such as commitment, preference, feasibility, and controllability, all of

*I would like to publically acknowledge my debt to four people, two whose written works have significantly influenced my thinking in a direct and striking way, Alice Rivlin who is one of the most perceptive and balanced of the practitioners of new rationalism, and Donald Campbell whose works on social experimentation and quasi-experimentation are classics of social science; and two people on the OSU campus from whom I have and hopefully will continue to learn much about how to structure knowledge for action, Dr. Saad Nagi and Dr. Phillip Burgess, both Mershon Professors of Public Policy.

which raise such questions as evaluation for what, evaluation for whom, evaluation with what impact on whom?

Moreover, I would argue that in evaluation or other forms of knowledge for action, the action that structures the knowledge side of the relationship has primacy over the knowledge that structures the action side of the relationship. Moreover, the ancients and medievalists generally affirmed this relationship—one we seem to have forgotten—namely, that this relationship distinguishes philosophy and science—which seek truth and reliability about knowing objects and their interrelationships—from technology—which seeks results and reliability about knowing how to do or make.

I am not raising here the question of the relative value of philosophy, science, and technology either for the individual or society as a whole. Rather, I am saying two things; that program evaluation—like any technology—is not science, and it is not useful to deal with it as if it were; and further, that program evaluation is not entirely a derivative of science nor the application of science, and it is again not useful to deal with it as if it were. Thus, in my judgment, the questions raised about evaluation *for what, for whom, and with what impact on whom* are the primary questions and should determine the evaluation design as well as the methods used to implement that design such as what you want to measure, how you want to measure, etc.

A third theme of my reference to knowledge for action which I would like you to consider is that the knowledge to action or knowledge-guiding-action side of the relationship may or may not be helpful in the action-guiding-knowledge process. Another way to put this is that analysis—good, solid "scientifically" respectable evaluation analysis—which is not structured by the action requirements may not be useful and may even be harmful in approaching action. Briefly consider the following three illustrations, examples which apply whether we're talking about social system performance, policy evaluation, program evaluation, or even individual performance evaluation.

First, I can find very little evidence to support the proposition that evaluation analysis leads to commitment or decision to act or to determining the basic direction of an action; rather, evaluation serves to give structure to and to specify the content of the act once a commitment is made. On the other hand, some evidence exists for the proposition that evaluation analysis can pre-empt or otherwise prevent commitment to an act or its basic direction and more evidence that it can be systematically used to avoid a commitment.

Second, consider what might be called the "problem/analysis fallacy," i.e., the notion that understanding the problem is essential to discovering a solution. On the one hand, we have numerous examples of techniques and processes which work, we know they work, we can successfully predict conditions under which they will work, and yet we have little understanding why. On the other hand, we have numerous examples of problems for which analysis has identified and delineated causes, for which, not surprisingly, corresponding solutions have not been discovered or created.

Finally, it appears to me that the use of evaluation analysis tends to weight the reliable over the relevant. That is, the fact that evaluation analysis tends to base its conclusions on those factors which are quantifiable and measurable occurs often enough to question whether the practice is not endemic to the analysis rather than an abuse of the techniques, as its proponents claim.

What I have been trying to say is that the purpose of all evaluation is to improve performance and generate solutions—not to identify problems. To the degree that evaluation fails to do this, to that degree it is not good evaluation. I think most of us would agree with the conclusions of Alice Rivlin, namely, that systematic evaluation has led to little performance improvement, that program evaluation has not led to improved programs.[1] Though Rivlin has some excellent concrete suggestions for overcoming some of these deficiencies, and in spite of the fact that her's is one of the most useful books on this whole issue, Rivlin's treatment fails, in my judgment, to identify the major reason for the failure of program evaluation, for the source of the problem lay not primarily in the techniques of evaluation but in the failure to let the purpose, namely, to improve performance in the context of demands and constraints of achieving that purpose—structure the design, content, and process of evaluation.

Let me list some broad illustrative guidelines arising from this notion of the action purpose of program evaluation in order to clarify what I mean by action directing knowledge. For example, if the purpose of evaluation is to influence policy or program decisions, then it will focus on policy variables, that is, on those factors or events over which there is some control.

In addition, the evaluation (and the evaluator) has to address itself to the questions of clients and the questions of social leverage. By clients, I mean those who will utilize the evaluation. It is important to make some distinction here between clients and sponsors. A sponsor of evaluation is someone who pays the bill either in money or prestige. A client is the decision-maker who needs the information. The Office of Education may be a sponsor of school district program audits; it is *not* the primary *client* because it is not the primary user. Moreover, many program evaluations have multiple users—policy-makers, change agents, managers, operators such as social workers, the public, or the consumer of the services. Not only should the evaluation speak to points to which the various client users can respond, it must speak to them within the constraints within which they can make decisions.

The questions which must be answered in order to make decisions is a function not only of the system or program being evaluated, but also of the manner in which a public issue is defined and the social leverage which a decision-maker has. Thus, for example, any evaluation must be structured within the context of expected levels of achievements or expected levels of expenditures. This question of client affects everything from the selection of outputs and their measurement, to the selection of reporting requirements. (It has always been interesting to me, for example, that evaluation reports are usually (a) written and (b) lengthy in spite of the fact that most decision-makers have little time to read.)

Examined this way, the issue is not what the *user* needs or the evaluator *thinks* he needs, *but what the user thinks he needs.* A performance evaluation which utilizes 200 variables, for example, is much less likely to be useful than one which utilizes 5. In this regard, the issue is not what constitutes evidence or what the evaluator thinks constitutes evidence, but *what constitutes evidence for the user.* For example, the computation of social benefits in terms of dollar costs may be a very sophisticated evaluation technique but it is highly unlikely that a decision-maker will attend to such information. Finally, and most obviously, program evaluators should identify their clients and have close ties with them in order to understand their needs and this may be best achieved by involving them in the task development stage of the evaluation design. While this approach may conflict with the prevailing notions of the need for independent assessment, the "not invented here syndrome," the "intellectural Bwanaism syndrome" (the missionary to native or expert to worker approach), and the "intellectual Brahminism syndrome" (the "I'll convince him my idea is his ideas," or the humble expert approach) make the absence of client participation in the design stage an even greater problem in my opinion.

The social leverage issue noted above has several elements beyond the existence of a client and the control the client has over a problem—namely, the nature of the problem, the need, and the anticipated program deficiency. First of all, the kinds of problems or deficiencies which evaluation should seek to address or identify are those which correspond to available *ameliorative* resources. To use an elementary example, it is rather fruitless to point out to a manager that a major weakness of a program is that its professional personnel do not have master's degrees if the average salary which the organization can afford is $10,000 per year and the city budget director is in the process of laying off personnel because of cutbacks in Federal Programs. Secondly, evaluation should focus on problems that are inherently *tractable*, that is, problems which can be defined in ways which can provide the opportunity for discovering partial compensatory, ameliorative, and preventive solutions which do not totally impede progress towrd some systematic solution. Finally, evaluations should focus if possible on *multiplier effects*, either potential high productivity improvement areas or high cost reduction areas.

Let me conclude my remarks on this first point by protecting my flank, i.e., by trying to clarify what I'm *not* saying. Evaluation research and analysis are not action, they are knowledge. So, their purpose is to lead to improvements by identifying feasible ways and means—not to make decisions. Thus, I am not saying that evaluation and particularly evaluation analysis be structured to arrive at pre-selected solutions or to mask ideologically-based value judgments. I am not arguing for advocacy research and analysis, though I'll have something to say about that later, but for directly useful research. Discovery is still the purpose of evaluation, and evaluation analysis, unlike propaganda, involves the discovery of what can be done and in an instrumental sense, what ought to be done in relation to purpose, and how to do it.

EXPERIMENTAL EVALUATION—
ACTION FOR KNOWLEDGE

Turning now to my second major point—namely, that systematic experimentation has substantial advantages over post-hoc evaluation analysis relative to improving social services and that reflecting on the problems of experimental design analysis may help to improve evaluation analysis—I would like to use Rivlin's book as a straw man once again. Experimentation, to paraphrase Rivlin, is systematic action for social knowledge.

First, broad definitions will help to clarify what I mean. There are a variety of techniques referred to as program evaluation. For example, there is descriptive evaluation or what I call input evaluation. When you ask the conference director how the program is going and the answer is "great, 400 people registered and all 4 speakers showed up"—that's input evaluation. Or, there is what people call process evaluation. If the answer is, "Oh hell, last night's session started an hour late and the microphone didn't work for the final speaker"—that's process evaluation. Then, there's output evaluation, which can take a number of forms. If the answer is "30 people have asked to have a similar symposium next month," that's output analysis. If the answer is that 30 people have asked to have an additional workshop on Wednesday provided that Lou Higgs didn't attend, the conference moderators would be asked to moderate the sessions, and the commentators would be asked to summarize and comment on the workshop discussions, that's what Robert Walker calls "accountability evaluation,"[2] i.e., where the feedback is structured so that each individual's contribution is clearly known and the consequences can be equitably and differentially provided. Finally, there is the natural experiment which simply refers to input-output analysis of an on-going program which is done according to valid statistical design techniques.

There are also a variety of meanings for the word experiment in the social action field. For example, there are models and simulations—of the paper and pencil, computer, or laboratory types—which are called experiments and in which experiment is used in the knowledge sense. There are the "try it, you'll like it" experiments—what Rivlin called the Random Innovations—so prevalent in the 60's in which experiment is used in the common sense meaning of "something new." There are demonstrations which are essentially social intervention programs with built-in evaluation techniques. Sometimes, as mentioned above, the word natural experiment is used to designate the application of sophisticated evaluation techniques to either random innovation or demonstrations. Obviously, it is clear that evaluation is more likely to be productive when a program is designed so that it can be evaluated.

Finally, there is what Rivlin calls "systematic experiments" what the NSF Experimental R&D Program, designed and staffed primarily by Physical Scientists and Engineers, calls real world testing, and what Life and Social Sciences have called field or clinical experiments. Donald Campbell and his colleagues at Northwestern call it "experimental evaluation"[3] and distinguish between experiments and quasi-experiments basically on the degree of experimental control involved in the design.

Systematic experiments are simply the attempt to apply the experimental method of science to social intervention. Briefly recall some of the major aspects of experimental design. Basically the elements of the design are simple—some defined and measured treatments (independent variables) are delivered in a controlled way under controlled conditions, and measured observations of the intervention on the experimental unit or subject are taken. There are a variety of experimental and quasi-experimental designs, but the basic elements are the experimental controls which are used to insure internal validity—that is, attributability of results to the independent variables,—and external validity—namely, the generalizability or applicability of results across subjects and situations. The basic forms of control are randomization, blocking or matching pairs of homogeneous units, factorial designs for interaction analysis, and control groups.

As Rivlin and others point out, the failure of post-hoc program evaluation or non-experimental program evaluation to make progress in evaluating social programs, and particularly in learning how to produce better programs is not entirely the fault of evaluation analysis techniques or the analysts. In great measure, it is a function of two things. First, that programs are usually not designed with evaluation in mind. Even if they are, the primary purpose is *to do* things, *not to learn* things; hence, there are inevitably serious if not insurmountable data problems. Second, and perhaps most important, because the programs are primarily action programs, both success and operational requirements mean that steps will be taken and decisions made which inevitably tend to diminish the basis for sound and reliable analysis.

One solution then is to undertake experiments, that is, to design programs primarily to produce knowledge, to test and measure program effectiveness. As Rivlin states it, "until systematic experimentation is undertaken on a significant scale, the prospects seem dim indeed for learning how to produce better service." My first point was not meant to imply that post-hoc evaluation was not a valuable tool, but rather that it needed to be strengthened by making it more responsive to the action requirements. In a similar fashion, this second point does not mean to imply that systematic experimentation is a panacea which can supplant post-hoc evaluation analysis, but rather that it is a valuable supplemental tool.

Systematic experimentation has many problems—technical, administrative, political and ethical—and in many cases will neither be the most feasible nor the most valuable form of evaluation. I will discuss the technical problems below in some detail. Let me now say a few words about the others.

The administrative and organization problems are substantial and essentially they boil down to creating an environment conducive to innovation, self-renewal and change, and a substantial commitment to planning and supervision—all traditionally looked upon as overhead costs. Suffice it to say that I don't believe the organizational design problems to be as difficult as some people believe. I have seen them overcome; I have overcome them myself. Ralph Widner[4] calls the management of such problems strategic as opposed to maintenance bureaucracy and the primary requisite is the *sine qua non* of all good management, faith that it can be done and guts to do it.

The political problems are another matter. Experimentation is risky, but in great part that is a function of the scale, visibility, and the intensity of the experiment. Secondly, by its very nature, the experiment is unequitable in the distinction of benefits. This is particularly a problem in the social sciences when a successful experiment "will do good things." The ethical questions are also tough ones, as evidenced by the whole body of regulations and procedures coming into being relative to experimenting with human subjects. My response to these problems is that moral and political problems exist in almost all areas of endeavor and obviously constrain behavior. But, I see no basic political and moral problems which prohibit a sensible use of experimentation, and a number of useful and productive arenas in which these constraints either are not serious or can be substantially mitigated.

Before moving to a consideration of the technical constraints (which, in my judgment, are vastly overrated), I want to reiterate my basic theme up to this point. I suggested earlier that program evaluation should primarily seek action-structured knowledge. My second point states that a primary means to that knowledge is knowledge-structured action—that is, action for knowledge, action whose purpose, direction, planning, decisions, structure, and functions should all be structured and directed by the knowledge requirements. The corollary of this second point is that the knowledge requirements are the same knowledge requirements described under the first point, namely, knowledge for action—technological knowledge not scientific knowledge. Most of the technical problems of experimentation pointed out by Rivlin and most of Campbell's descriptions of the difficulties of experimentation and even quasi-experimentation arise from treating experimentation as if it were a scientific enterprise rather than a scientific technology adapted to technological rather than scientific purposes. Perhaps some concrete illustration would be helpful.

The emphasis on controls, their necessity, and the problems of the lack of control all arise from a bias toward scientific criteria of evidence and certitude rather than from a decision-maker's bias which is relative and comparative—in relation to the certitude of other alternatives and the degree of benefit vis-a-vis current practice. Likewise the problem of replication and the problem of sampling are primarily a function of the need for generalizability. Science strives for and values generalizability. Technology needs only generablizability that falls within the scope of the decision-maker, the function to be performed, or the decision to be made. If I'm evaluating a program within the Franklin County Welfare Department, I don't need to know whether or not the Franklin County is representative. The argument is made that experimentation is a demanding form of evaluation. But the same argument can be made for post-hoc evaluation. The demands referred to come from the demands for statistical rigor and many of these demands are pseudo-demands in regard to action research. Experimentation is an extraordinarily good technical tool for specialized program evaluation and individual performance evaluation because the homogeneity of the units is high and the need for generalizability low.

Let me digress a moment on this whole question of statistical experimental design and statistical analysis, particularly on the question of sampling and other forms of statistical control. The crucial question in sampling is the definition of the population, that is, the selection of those factors or variables by which the population is defined. In the theory of experimental design, of course, the question of heterogeneity or homogeneity and the question of representativeness are supposed to refer to critical factors. Unfortunately, few advocates of statistical evaluation or experimental design will admit that we have very little relevant theory and hence the selection of critical factors and therefore the definition of a population as well as the determination of homogeneous or heterogeneous units is, at best, arbitrary. In fact, what happens most often is that these questions are determined by the data base rather than by theory. For example, if we want to anayze the effects of the Model Cities Program, we not only have very little theory that tells us that, for example, population size may be a critical variable of the subject pool, we have even less theory to telling us what the unit size for homogeneous units ought to be. Yet, I would be willing to bet that nine out of ten evaluators would use size rather than complexity of city organization as a sampling criteria, and I would even wager more that the size of the unit categories were readily adaptable from categories used by the census bureaus.

My point is not to criticize these choices but simply to stress that experimental designs and statistical analysis are like all other information processing systems: they are extremely dependent on a-priori and often arbitrary coding systems, systems derived from the purposes of the information system itself. If the categories are arbitrary, then the categories should be selected not only by the purposes of the decision-maker but by his priorities too.

Now the purposes of the decision-maker are usually time dependent and the question he typically asks is, "Does this alternative work better than what I'm now doing or better than the other alternatives I've got?" This suggests, it seems to me, four broad guidelines. First, most experimentation ought to be comparative—i.e., experimental design ought to provide evidence regarding the *relative* performance of *different* alternatives of configurations rather than simple tests of the treatment effects of a single alternative or program. Second, that replication is very important not for generalizability, i.e., to insure the external validity of results but rather to insure reliability—that the experiment was properly conducted. Third, we ought to create experimental programs that are rich enough in their data collection to provide differing levels of reliable evidence that correspond to the different levels of information needs that are derived from the different levels among priorities affirmed by the decision-maker.

Fourth, the experimentor or experimental evaluator should have stakes independent of the client and the subjects of the experiment. This is not inconsistent with earlier administrations about client involvement and participation in evaluation task definition process. Rather, it refers to the political problem of cheating and the technical problem of allowing an experiment to "degenerate" into an action program rather than a learning program. Perhaps a brief description of the rationale for the NSF and NBS Experimental Incentives Programs and how they were structured within the government will serve to illustrate this point.

These two programs arose out of the recognition of a very serious national economic problem which manifested itself in a variety of forms. One manifestation was the growing seriousness of the balance of trade problem. Another was the problem of productivity which affected the balance of trade problem, the domestic economy, and the general quality of life—especially in regard to the service sector, both public and private. A third was the shift in national priorities from military and space to domestic civil sector problems and the tremendous concomitant transition costs as manifested in terms of serious unemployment of a highly paid, highly trained core of professional scientists and engineers and the resulting loss to the consumer economy. Pressures increased for economic and social reasons for a push to transfer technology and technological capability. Among the catalysts were a White House Task Force on Technological Goals and the Kennedy Bill (Senate Bill 32) calling for a massive civil science and technology program with a funding base of approximately 1.6 billion dollars.

The White House took the position that we simply do not have enough understanding of how to do the job; accordingly, they recommended a policy research program to evaluate the potency of various Federal options. The organizational elements of this program are interesting. First of all, the monies are specifically earmarked for experimentation. Second, both the NSF and NBS programs are ad hoc with a limited duration. Third, only experimental money is included in the programs, that is, neither NSF or NBS will have follow-through money to fund operating programs that the experimental evaluations show to be effective. Finally, the programs were given to NSF and NBS precisely because they are research — not mission — agencies. All of these factors are aimed at insuring that the evaluator has no stake in the success of the experimental program being tested.

Prototyping: Knowledge into Action

Now, my third and final major point, namely, that experimentation can be viewed and often conducted as part of an architectural and engineering design process in contrast to a scientific research endeavor. Most of my basic thinking relative to this point originated in my experience in trying to utilize social science in the military R&D business. Under the leadership of such people as Dr. Tom Milburn, now a Mershon Professor of OSU, and Dr. Richard Snyder, now Director of the Mershon Program of OSU, we were trying to develop political, social, and economic criteria for evaluating strategic policy, force postures and weapons. My thinking was substantially expanded by my experience with Dr. Philip Burgess of OSU when we served as co-Directors of a project to develop and demonstrate a prototype planning and decision information system for the Governor of Puerto Rico in 1971—a project discussed in a joint paper presented to the 1972 Annual Meeting of the National Governor's Conference.[5]

Additional refinements of that basic thinking have come

from our efforts to develop a community research plan for the City of Columbus which included the need for a Community Social Conditions Profile and a Community Social Services Profile last summer and fall. The version I will present here contains still further refine made by Burgess based on his efforts to develop a Columbus Area Social Report and are articulated in much greater detail and undoubtedly in much greater clarity in a chapter by Burgess and Richard Conway entitled "Public Goods and Social Mobilization; A Multi-Stage, Multi-Method Investigation of the Theory of Collective Action," to be published in a forthcoming volume of the Sage Series in Public Policy.[6]

What I would like to present to you is the outline of a different synthesis of the knowledge-action relationships presented earlier and both a research and action strategy that flow from it. The basic premise of this synthesis is the design or innovation perspective, that is, the conception of the policy-making process as a design problem and the conception of the decision-maker as a designer in the context of a multi-stage decision process. In this view, policy making involves designing new states of affairs or adapting to current states of affairs in response to a changing internal structure [needs] and/or a changing environment i.e., new challenges or opportunities. Multi-stage decision processes might be contrasted with goal-oriented models of the traditional public administration or the new systematic-analysis and the model of incrementalism advanced by Lindblom and others and lies somewhere between the two poles. It assumes like the traditional and systems models that desired end states are knowable, yet—unlike the traditional model—*goal-setting* and *implementation* are viewed as quite distinguishable parts of the process, for one can never know—given the range of uncertainties—how he is going to reach his goal. Hence, like incrementalism, multi-stage decision processes involve a continuing process of charting and recharting one's course, but—unlike incrementalism—the desired end state is known and maintained throughout to guide the process of charting and the process of steering, adapting, and adjusting to changing conditions.

Consequently, a multi-stage decision process involves a continuing process of design and redesign, incorporates a view of man and his environment akin to Simon's notions in the *Sciences of the Artificial,*[7] and involves the following process:

1. First, the actor takes his present position as a given;
2. Next, he articulates a goal, a desired end-states;
3. Third, he employs successive approximations each designed to bring him closer to his objective when each successive approximation improves performance; and
4. Throughout the process he obeys the injunction: "Do the best you can from where you are."

If the policy maker is a designer or innovator, then the policy researcher must take on the tasks of developing design theories for innovation that can be used in the process of social system design and he utilizes the same decision process just articulated.

An additional research or experimental strategy to evaluative analysis or experimental designs discussed above might be called a *prototyping strategy* and differs substantially from the hypothesis testing experiment described above. The prototype involves designing a program or program improvement based on the best knowledge available from theory, experience, post-hoc evaluations, etc. Unlike the experiment from which conclusions are drawn from performance differences under different treatment conditions, the prototype draws conclusions from intensive analysis and evaluation of a deliberately designed, on-going operation against hypotheses, expectations and hunches explicitly developed during the design phase of the prototype. In other words, prototyping is an approach to social innovation that moves from theory to policy guidance, that treats research and development as a continuous and interative process of theory elaboration and corroboration, and social policy as a continuous and interative process of approximations to desired end-states where each successive approximation improves performance.

We are now talking about a new and different relationship of knowledge and action. Now we are talking about the knowledge *into* action, theory into practice—which I initially suggested de-emphasizing. And the synthesis is treating both the decision-process and the research process as a *technological* process which starts from a specified end state but whose strategy is determined by theory. Now we have a designer/decision-maker matched by a designer-investigator. Thus, this prototyping is a knowledge to action strategy. Let me briefly outline the stages of a broad knowledge to action strategy which moves from conditions of high control and low generalizability (e.g., laboratory experiments) to conditions of low control and high generalizability (e.g., prototypes).

The first step is to identify a theory thought to be relevant to a social problem. The next step is to specify end-states, that is, research goals. In short, prototyping requires attention to the development of engineering models in social analysis by applying a design perspective in which the goal is the development of design specifications for public policy. The third step requires the development of a multi-stage research strategy that applies multiple analytical and inferential methods to the exploration and corroboration of expected behaviors derived from theory. Multiple methods are invoked to avoid confirmation on the basis of a single kind of evidence. The strategy is multi-stage because the designer-investigator attempts to build on each prior stage of research as he designs subsequent stages. Most important in this regard is the notion that each successive stage in the prototyping research strategy should increasingly relax the ceteris paribus conditions that are inherent in the formal models and simulations that give expression to the theory under examination.

The first stage in this multi-stage research strategy is to develop a formal model(s) specifying design implications of that theory. The second is to develop laboratory experiments and simulations which test specific assertions flowing from the theory and formal model. The great advantage of both formal modeling and laboratory experimentation lies in the degree of control that can be exerted over the research. Such research minimizes the problem of extraneous, uncontrolled variation confounding the results that are obtained. In the formal model and the well-designed laboratory experiment, the investigator can adjust parameters and treatments in almost any way that the creative or investigative impulse dictates. In addition, the investigator can be relatively certain that the variation which does arise is a function of his manipulation alone (plus measurable error). In this type of research, control and internal validity are both high and extraneous, uncontrolled variation is minimal.

However, the very advantages of the controlled laboratory setting and the elaborations from formal modeling are the sources of their disadvantages—the research setting is unnatural. It is precisely the absence of the empirical richness that denies the researcher the confidence he might otherwise have with respect to the transfer potential of his findings to the domain where the findings ultimately are to be applied.

Hence, the next step in the prototyping strategy involves a test of the theory in a more natural field setting where control diminishes somewhat but where empirical richness and hence generalizability increase. In this setting, the designer-investigator can avoid the sterile atmosphere of the laboratory. Quasi-experimental field studies and social surveys enable the investigator to examine the effects of contextual factors that might have some bearing on the research conducted, on the theory giving rise to the research, and on any policy guidance that might be derived from research. At the same time, the quasi-experimental nature of the research still insures that some control can be exerted over the research.

A formal prototype concludes the final stage in the prototyping strategy. The design of the prototype uses the findings and knowledge garnered from previous research and applies it to a planned, controlled, relatively small social intervention. The advantage of the formal prototype lies in the richness of the research setting and the ability of the researcher to monitor his manipulation of a real world environment owing to the substantial knowledge of the operation of causal factors gained from earlier stages in the process. If all the research findings are in the same direction, substantial credence can be given to policy guidance based on the research and the designer-investigator will be more confident in making recommendations as well as the decision-maker more confident in following them. This is not, however, an end to the strategy being advocated, for all policies should be subjected to continuing appraisal and re-design. However, policy appraisal and revision—or, if appropriate, termination— are often difficult to achieve when the institution administering the policy is committed to its success. Ideally, the execution of an innovation from guidance based on research would itself be viewed as an experiment, one whose impact was constantly being monitored, appraised, and evaluated—just as Rivlin and others have suggested that in addition to capitalizing on random and natural innovations, we should begin systematic experimentation with alternative social policies in areas of major concern.

Feedback gained from continuing appraisal and assessment—which, by the way, will utilize systematic analysis and may utilize quasi-scientific experimentation—can be used both in the redesign of innovations and in the further elaboration of social theory. Such a perspective not only makes policy sensitive to the acid test of implementation, but also facilitates the adaptation of policy through time via a continuous process of redesign. This larger cyclical process is depicted in Figure 1.

Figure 1: The Multiple Stages of Prototyping Research Strategy*

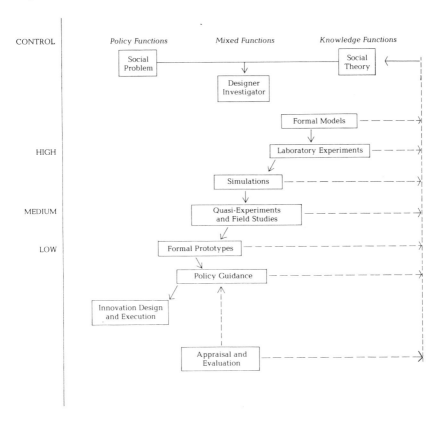

* This chart and the text on pages 99-103 were adopted from (1) Burgess, Philip M. and Louis D. Higgs, "Science, Policy, and the Utilization of Social Technology," paper prepared for The National Governors Conference meeting in San Juan in September, 1972, and (2) Burgess, Philip M. and Richard Conway, Public Goals and Voluntary Associations: A Multi-Stage Investigation of Collective Action in Labor Union Locals, (Beverly Hills: Sage Publications, Inc., 1973).

The primary difference between the knowledge to action strategy suggested here and the typical process of scientific experimentation is the latter's concern for eliminating all plausible competing explanations of the results obtained. The designer/decision-maker is not sensitive to competing explanations. If his works, that is, if his theory yields specifications for policy which in turn yield the desired results, he is satisfied. His curiosity is not such that he is compelled to worry about competing explanations, just as the engineer is not worried that outmoded, pre-Einsteinian physics will nevertheless help him develop reliable specifications for building a bridge or skyscraper.

In other words, it seems to me that even when we do talk about knowledge to action, we tend to fall back on traditional, conventional, and largely irrelevant scientific criteria for evaluating the quality of the knowledge we want to imvoke in the process of designing more responsive public policies.

Footnotes for Chapter 4

[1] Alice M. Rivlin, *Systematic Thinking for Social Action.*(Washington, D. C.: The Brookings Institute, 1971).

[2] Robert A. Walker, "The Ninth Panacea: Program Evaluation." *Evaluation*, Vol. 1, No. 1 (1972), pp. 45-53.

[3] Donald Campbell and Julian Stanley, *Experimental and Quasi-Experimental Design for Research* (Chicago: Rand-McNally, 1963).

[4] Ralph Widner, "Regional Instiutions for Improving the Public Utilization of Techology," *Conference on Technology and Social Institutions* (Engineering Foundation, 1973).

[5] Philip M. Burgess and Louis D. Higgs, "Science, Policy, and the Utilization of Social Technology" Paper prepared for The National Governors Conference meeting in San Juan in September, 1972.

[6] Philip M. Burgess and Richard Conway, *Public Goals and Voluntary Associations: A Multi-Stage Investigation of Collective Action in Labor Union Locals* (Beverly Hills: Sage Publications, Inc., 1973).

[7] Herbert A. Simon, *Sciences of the Artificial,*(Cambridge: MIT Press, 1969).

COMMENTARY

Herbert S. Parnes

To the extent that I have captured his meaning, it appears to me that Dr. Higgs' objective of being provocative has been fulfilled. Reading his paper has caused me to rethink my own position on evaluating social programs. I find much in the paper with which I agree; but several aspects of it are subject to criticism.

Part of the problem is created at the very outset. Higgs professes the intention of discussing "the nature of evaluation and its relation to other forms of human activity." Yet one of the gaps I find in the paper is its failure to explore the several dimensions of evaluation. There are a number of quite different perspectives in which a social program can be "evaluated," and which type of evaluation one has in mind conditions what can be said about the evaluation process. For example, at the very simplest level one may ask whether the intended beneficiaries of a program are better off than they would be without it. Alternatively, one may ask whether, given the objectives of a program, its effects are being accomplished in the most efficient manner. Third, one may raise the question whether, all things considered, society is better off with the program than without it, i.e., whether the benefit-cost ratio exceeds unity. Finally, the most complex and at the same time the most meaningful question that one may raise in a planning context is whether, given the limited resources and the multitude of objectives that society has, the particular program is the best one that might have been undertaken. To use Alice Rivlin's example, shall we educate the poor or cure cancer? Conceptually, in the jargon of cost-benefit analysis, what is indicated here is the necessity of equalizing benefit-cost ratios at the margin for all social investments.

Now, in the context of these different meanings of evaluation, let us consider Higgs' first major point, which comes in two parts: (1) that evaluation is an indispensable part of sound planning, decision making, and management and (2) that the evaluation process is ascientific and inevitably political. That evaluation is part of the planning and decision-making process is unquestionably true for all of the types of evaluation that I have enumerated, but it should be noted that there is considerable difference in the locus of the decision-making power depending upon which type of evaluation one is talking about. If the question is the first to which I have referred the decision may lie in the hands of an administrator; if it is the fourth, the decision must be taken at the highest level of policy making in the society.

Irrespective of what type of evaluation one is talking about, Higgs' contention that the process is ascientific and inevitably political seems to me to be only half true. Every evaluation of a course of action inevitably involves two distinct intellectual processes: (1) an analysis of the consequences of the action and (2) a judgment, all things considered, as to whether those consequences are good or bad. The first process is by no means ascientific. It involves the type of question with respect to which scientific method is completely relevant. The second process, of course, involves a question with respect to which scientific method is not relevant and cannot be made to be. I agree with Higgs that there is danger in misdirected scientism; in making cost-benefit analyses, many economists have been guilty of "weighting the quantifiable over the relevant," to use Higgs' words. But this surely provides no ground for the opposite error of arguing that the total evaluation process should be, or indeed can be, ascientific.

Higgs' second major point is that systematic experimentation has substantial advantages over post-hoc evaluative analysis and that opportunities for experimental evaluation ought to be built into social programs. Both of these points, I believe, are good ones. Yet—as Higgs acknowledges—experimentation is not always possible, or at least not socially desirable for ethical reasons. Thus, one does not wish to preclude the possibility of advocating post-hoc evaluative analysis. Furthermore, as Donald Campbell has shown, with appropriate ingenuity researchers can go far toward extending the logic of laboratory experimentation into settings not fully experimental.

Higgs third major point is that "experimentation can be viewed and often conducted as part of an architectural and engineering design process in contrast to a scientific research endeavor." He advocates a multi-stage decision-making process in which the existing position is taken as given and a goal is articulated which is then approached in successive approximations. I have no problem in accepting this, but it is not at all clear to me that this approach obviates the need for scientific method. Higgs argues that the difference between the scientist and the designer or decision-maker is that the former is concerned with "eliminating all plausible competing explanations of the results obtained" whereas the latter is concerned only with whether his approach "works," i.e., yields the desired results. But this formulation blithely ignores the crucial question of the kind of evidence required to decide whether something "works."

To state my position in a nutshell: whether one is a traditional planner or an incrementalist, to evaluate a program requires knowledge of what its consequences are. This is not, of course, a sufficient basis for evaluation but it is a necessary one; and in ascertaining consequences I know of no substitute for the scientific method, which attempts to uncover the true independent relationships among variables. To put it simply, in evaluating a training program I want to be sure that the lower unemployment I observe among its graduates is indeed attributable to their having been through the program rather than to their having been brighter or more highly motivated to begin with. In this sense, I must always be concerned for eliminating all plausible competing explanations for the results obtained.

COMMENTARY

Clyde W. Franklin, Jr.

"Experimental Design in Social Intervention Programs: Some Perspectives on Evaluation" is a provocative paper which has been written on a topic of vital concern to many social scientists in academic and non-academic circles. The author is to be commended for identifying and exploring this increasingly important problem area in the social and behavioral sciences. Moreover, recognition should also be extended for his courageous efforts to "reject substantial parts of the conventional wisdom of the new scientism or new rationalism" in calling for a "more balanced interaction between knowledge and action and a proper sequencing of the interaction."

To begin with, the paper under scrutiny was developed around three major points:

1) That evaluation, as a part of sound planning, decision-making and management, is a tool ultimately and primarily for action and therefore, should be scientific and inevitably political;
2) that systematic experimentation or quasi-experimentation has substantial advantages over evaluative analysis relative to social services improvement and viewing evaluation through the experimental perspective and the problems of evaluating experiments sheds some useful light on the problems of evaluations and how to cope with them; and finally,
3) that experimentation can be viewed and often conducted as part of an architectural and engineering design process rather than as a quasi-scientific endeavor.

Each of the above points and its implications are examined.

The assertion that "evaluation is a planning, decision-making and management tool whose purpose is to develop knowledge for action" seems sound and is not questioned. To be sure, such action processes as commitment, preference, feasibility, and so forth are to be considered in evaluation; and, some researchers would easily incorporate them into any analysis or evaluation. However, Mr. Higgs appears to have extended the above point to include a different type of analysis for evaluation research—one that is basically humanistically oriented and simultaneously produces results and reliability. Showing a preference for this type of analysis, he suggests that while his strategy does not seek truth and reliability about knowing objects and their relationships, it, nevertheless, seems more amenable to evaluation research. The major points stressed in the original paper are "that action does and should structure and guide the process of acquiring and refining knowledge"; "that action which structures the knowledge side of the relationship has primacy over the knowledge that structures the action side of the relationship"; "that the questions raised about evaluation for what, for whom, and with what impact on whom are the primary questions and should determine the evaluation design as well as the methods used to implement that design"; "that analysis which is not structured by the action requirements may not be useful and may even be harmful in approaching action"; and finally, "that the use of evaluation analysis tends to weight the reliable over the relevant."

A cursory examination of the above statements and their rationales reveals that stated differences between the approaches to evaluation research are unconvincing and if contrasts can be drawn, they very well may be a function of knowledge utilization and/or application rather than inherent discrepancies. For instance, there is nothing implicit in questions about evaluation involving "for what," "for whom," and "with what" that would dictate a "nonscientific" approach. As Herbert Blumer has so eloquently stated, "the genuine mark of an empirical science is to respect the nature of its empirical world" and these questions are a part of the empirical world. In other words, because evaluation analysis may not in the past have led to commitment or decision to act should not be interpreted as reflective of the strategy potential. Instead, one may wish to question the *users* of evaluation analysis with respect to the adequacy of their pragmatic orientations.

The first point adumbrated in the paper under consideration is interesting in that there are explicit implications for the relationship between explanation, prediction and control. To imply that prediction can occur without explanation means very little other than stunted empiricism. In other words, I suggest that solutions are at best incomplete unless explanation, prediction and control are conspicuous features of evaluation. In addition, while the argument presented by Higgs would suggest that systematic evaluation fails because purpose does not guide strategy, it *is* possible to explore the cause of failure in a vein which would imply failure as a consequence of incongruence between evaluation analysis and application. Thus the problem may not be generic to evaluation analysis but rather, due to coordination of evaluation and application.

A final point to be made at this juncture deals with the production of solutions devoid of interest in problem specification. While it may be compelling to toy with the idea of producing solution after solution, ultimately there must be a linkage of solutions to problems if solutions are to be meaningful. Also, it would appear that "problems" should contribute to the direction of solutions unless one concedes that there are "unmoved movers."

The advantages of experimental evaluation over post-hoc evaluation analysis is the second major point developed in the paper being evaluated. Unfortunately, this section is presented in a fashion that makes it difficult for the reader to understand the experimental method of science should be applied to social intervention since Higgs does not feel that evaluation analysis is a science.

Additionally, while I remain somewhat partial to experimentation, it is not at all clear from the perspective presented why experimentation will produce superior results for action programs. While the author suggests that experiments can be designed primarily to produce knowledge, to test and to measure programs and so forth, no evidence is presented to show that survey designs could not produce similar results. To be certain, there are crucial distinctions to be made between the two methodological strategies and the necessity for such an explication can not be overemphasized. Succinctly, in a paper of this type, it is impossible to summarily dismiss the importance of technical discussions of internal and external validity as they relate to both experimentation and survey analysis.

The final major point explored by Higgs can be found in his section on "prototyping." An examination of this section reveals that "prototyping" is closely akin to what Clarence Schrag has referred to as a *theoretical* strategy—retroduction. Commensurately, it is implied that evaluation research needs to make advances in social theory to the extent that logical, empirical, operational and pragmatic adequacies are obtained. Yet, if one senses another line of thought permeating the Higgs paper, the impression is gleaned that Higgs is extraordinarily humanistic in his approach. This is apparent when he occasionally sounds very much like an enthnomethodologist and/or a phenomenologist. If this is a faithful assessment of the perspective, then there is a problem with major portions of the Higgs methodological presentation inasmuch numerous points expressed by Higgs are opposed diametrically to humanistic assumptions. Rectification of this problem would entail an advocation of softer methodological strategies such as the case study approach, deviant case analysis, analytic induction, participant observation, and so forth. The rationale for this position is that the complex array of interactions advanced by Higgs as characteristic of evaluation research cannot be ascertained via experimentation due to the obdurate character of the variable. Summarily, while the Higgs paper has been polemical and provocative, I remain unconvinced that perspectives on "evaluation research" have been enhanced.

CHAPTER 5

Alternative Models for Program Evaluation

Carol H. Weiss

Sooner or later, in any discussion of program evaluation and its utility for improving the quality of program services, the phrase "vested interests" comes up. The context is usually that agencies have vested interests in their jobs and in the services they give; boards of directors or legislatures or federal bureaucrats have vested interests in the interventions they support and on which they have staked their reputations. The relative ineffectiveness of program evaluation in *activating change* in programs—even when evaluative data clearly show that programs are not reaching their goals—is often explained away by hauling out a reference to vested interests.

Those of us in the business of program evaluation have our vested interests, too, and it's probably just as well to start out by putting them on the record. Our interests are in *information,* preferably valid information, and in the use of that information for decision-making. We believe in rationality—basing decisions about programs squarely on data about the effectiveness of programs.

And if we take a clear, cold look at just how useful and cost-effective program evaluation has been for improving service programs and delivery systems, we find that the record is hardly spectacular. Just as most human service programs have had indifferent success in improving the lot of clients, most program evaluations have had little impact on improving the quality of programs. Despite our high-flown rhetoric, evaluators share with program colleagues both the self-serving nature of the justification for our enterprise and the spotty record of success. It is, therefore, in a spirit of humility that I'd like to discuss some ways in which evaluation can become a more effective force in reshaping programs.

The purpose of evaluation is utilitarian. Its function is to provide evidence of the outcomes of programs so that wise decisions can be made about those programs in the future. To the extent that a program is achieving its goals, evaluative evidence supports continuation, expansion, increased allocations. But if evaluation discloses that a program is not achieving its goals, or achieving them only partially or for some groups, it should have something to say about future courses of action: should the program be shut down or cut back, or should it be modified and if so, in what ways. One of the problems with most program evaluations in the past is that they have been content to deliver over-all "go" or "no-go" assessments of program effectiveness with little attention to the implications for future action.

The theme of today's paper is that no one model of evaluation is suitable for all uses. Forcing all evaluations into a single mold, particularly the global mold that addresses the global question of how well the program is doing, can have perverse consequences. For evaluation even to have a chance of contributing to the rationalization of program decisions, it must know *first* what decisions have to be made. Second, it must contribute the types of data that will enable decision-makers to make wise choices in that context. Parenthetically, let us acknowledge that these are necessary but not sufficient conditions for actually improving the decisional choices that are made. My impression is that organizations also have to provide incentives and rewards for *using* evaluative information in decision-making.

What kinds of decisions do programs face? Essentially they are of three types: policy decisions, strategic (or managerial) decisions, and tactical decisions. Policy decisions are made at the highest level: should the program be continued or terminated, expanded or cut back, should a new program be undertaken and if so, what should it be like? Strategic decisions have to do with fundamental choices about modes of operation. Once the basic objectives are set, what methods should be followed to achieve those objectives? Which strategies of intervention should be continued, modified, or initiated, e.g., integration of services in centralized agencies or referral networks? Job training, job finding, or job making? Tactical decisions have to do with day-to-day program practices, choices about operating procedures. Only when the concrete decisions that face the program have been identified can evaluation be designed to yield usable information. If a program is going to be continued no matter what its failings— say, the United States Postal Service, it is fruitless to find out that it is ineffective on overall measures of success, but it can be productive to show what kinds of strategic modifications would improve its service. Likewise, if certain program strategies are invulnerable to change, such as classroom teaching or nursing home care for the elderly, there can be value in finding out whether there are better means to put the strategies into practice.

Given the premise that the pending decision should shape the evaluation, I'd like to discuss three evaluation models and the decisions for which they are suited. The three alternative models, and they by no means exhaust the list (although they may exhaust the time and the audience), are social experimentation, traditional evaluative research, and accountability systems. All of them deal in outcome data, evidence of the effectiveness of programs in attaining their goals, but each is apt for answering a different order of question and supplying information for a different type of decision.

I might note for the purposes of clarity that I'd like to confine the term "evaluation" to this meaning—the study of program effects in terms of the consequences, both intended and unintended, for the target groups and institutions. Like Roland Warren (See Chapter One) I have reservations about the contributions that social scientists can make at this time through evaluation research. In a period when most of the reformist program ideas that were accumulated over the past forty years have been tried and found wanting, further evaluation has its limits, and new conceptualizations and new modes of approach to problems are needed. I have come to believe that this is a time for the development of a new stock of intellectual capital. As social scientists we may be most effective by using our knowledge and our research and analytic skills to better understand the nature and career of social problems and to aid the *development* of program and policy.[1] But there is still a place for evaluation research, and the models I am discussing—social experiments, traditional evaluation, and accountability systems—are outcome evaluations.

Social Experiments

Social experiments are a way of planning rationally for the future. Unlike the backward stance of most evaluative efforts that survey the success of past programming, social experiments involve launching and testing prototypes of new ventures. Their function is to inform the policy-maker of the viability and effectiveness of innovations before he commits large amounts of money, time, and effort to a major national undertaking. Certainly the last decade has demonstrated that many program ideas that sound persuasive and even unimpeachable in principle, given our present state of knowledge, come a-cropper in operation. If policymakers can look at the consequences of a test run of a program before going gung-ho on a nationwide basis, they have the opportunity to reject the ineffective, improve the marginally effective, and mitigate the counter-productive side effects of new programs. It is for this type of major new policy decision that social experimentation is designed.

Social experiments are research. Their goal is to test. Their two basic features are: (1) they are true experiments, with random assignment of participants to program and control conditions, and with before and after measurement; and (2) the program is explicitly defined and firmly controlled, with the evaluation researchers responsible for ensuring that the program "stimulus" adheres to the prescribed principles and modes of operation. It is highly desirable for social experiments to be run in several sites with different external environments so that outcomes can be generalized over a range of conditions. Furthermore, if several variants of the basic program are run simultaneously, it is possible to gauge the effects of variations in treatment.

So long as social experiments were more a dream of beleaguered evaluators than a practical reality, they tended to emphasize the advantages and ignore possible limitations. The advantages, if all goes well, are delightful for the researcher and tremendously important for the decision-maker. With this kind of design, evaluation researchers can draw firm conclusions about the merit of a program. When they are dealing with true experiments, there is little uncertainty about whether it is the program or extraneous conditions that are causing the observed effects. When the program adheres to well-defined principles and procedures, there is little uncertainty about whether the program has had a fair test or whether its failings are the result of faulty administration or operation. When variants of the basic program are operated, there is information about the sets of conditions that have greater or lesser pay-off. The negative income tax experiments, housing allowance experiments, and health insurance experiments are recent and current examples. (It is probably not accidental that these current social experiments all involve direct payment of money. Money is easier to control than are services, which by their nature are subject to human differences.)

The recent experience has highlighted some of the difficulties as well. Social experiments are costly, because a prototype *program* has to be administered as well as a sophisticated research study. Usually it is possible to sample only a few sites, with a sacrifice in generalizability to other places and conditions. When the effects on small scattered groups of recipients are studied, the data may not be representative of outcomes that would have ensued if the program had saturated the areas. Furthermore, even when the researchers are in charge, program operations are not always well-handled, external conditions change, there are ethical problems in giving benefits to an experimental group (and not to controls) and then taking them away after the study is over. Long periods of time can elapse before the results become available for decisional purposes, and the reformist impetus that launched the experiment may have run out of steam.

Another limitation may be the seeming dearth of plausible new programs to test. Before a social experiment is launched, all the hard rational analysis that Roland Warren talked about last night has to be done: the nature of the social problem analyzed, its dynamics explored, the causal linkages hypothesized (or better yet, understood), effective points of intervention identified, the likelihood of successful intervention plausibly established, the political context for supporting and sustaining the intervention examined and found appropriate, and the likely benefits and the distribution of those benefits deemed sufficient to warrant the social cost. Social experimentaton will be useful for policymaking only when such analysis has generated a program or policy that is *worth* the testing. At this juncture, when a specific new social initiative is identified and has sufficient credibility to be considered by policymakers, social experimentation provides an elegant data base for decision-making. The kinds of information that it produces can prevent costly national failures and lead to better informed and more successful choices at the policy level.

Traditional Evaluation

Traditional evaluation is a catch-all term to describe the methods that have generally been used to study the effects of ongoing programs. Essentially I refer to before-after evaluation of the extent to which program goals are being realized, but under conditions that compromise the design. Usually the service imperatives of on-going programs preclude randomized assignment to experimental and control groups, and an approximation, such as "contrast groups," is resorted to. Further, the program is not under the evaluator's control so that the stimulus is imprecise and often wobbles around in response to internal and external opportunities and constraints. Traditional evaluation, if it is conducted with rigor and sophistication (and some luck), can give good estimates of overall program effectiveness for policy purposes. But given the constraints under which it often operates, it is perhaps better suited for other decisional needs. It is particularly appropriate for comparing the worth of alternative program strategies. Comparative study of the effects of different program components with different populations can yield evidence of what strategies work best with what groups. Variations in mode of operation and intensity of service can be tested as well. When federal administrators and program managers face decisions about whether to emphasize one set of methods or another, to scrap one technique and adopt a different one, the findings of traditional evaluation provide relevant information. (For detailed discussion, see Weiss, 1972.) By comparing the outcomes of variant approaches and program components within the context of the programs about which decisions will be made, evaluation demonstrates their relative work in the operating context and helps the decision-maker choose wisely. Since evaluation takes time and money, this approach is not likely to be worthwhile for assessing minor program features, but when choices of some magnitude are contemplated, it can make a significant contribution to the rationality of decision-making.

Accountability Systems

The last of the evaluation models that I will mention is a more recent (and still emergent) one—the accountability system. One of the pervasive problems with most past evaluations has been that they have been one-shot affairs. The evaluators come in, do a study of more or less elegance, and after their work is over, depart. But what about the rest of the time? Decisions still have to be made on a pretty regular basis on all kinds of matters—from policy questions regarding allocation of resources down to the nitty-gritty of intake criteria, staffing, hours of service, and so on. To meet continuing decisional needs, evaluative data can be built into an ongoing information system.

Most programs collect data, in fact often vast quantities of data, on clients, staff, finances, process, and plans. With the available computer technology, what used to be file cards in file boxes and file folders are now more likely to be computer files. Within the past decade, much effort has gone into turning the scattered bits and pieces of information, originally collected for a variety of different reasons, into comprehensive data systems for management use. But not many of the systems have included evaluative data, data on client outcomes, as part of the array. Sometimes this is not very hard to add. Even without the paraphernalia of computers, relatively simple measures of program success can be devised (e.g., job placement, maintenance of one's own home) and follow-up data collected on a systematic basis. With this input, the information system has the capability for analyzing a wide range of program conditions (e. g., length of service, referral flow, unit costs) against the types of client outcomes that ensued. If the data are selected and arranged with due care, such information can provide enormously useful guidance for decision-making on a regular basis. (But one thing we have learned is that program managers are likely to need some training in how to make best use of such information, both at the input and the output end.)

Here, then, is a possible evaluation-oriented information system. What makes it into an accountability system? Well, at the present time a variety of meanings inhabit the term "accountability system," and one will have to jostle out the others before the term can gain currency and usefulness. One useful meaning of accountability is that program data are so specified that each individual staff member or staff unit can be held accountable for its own performance. Data are produced showing the "success" record of each person or unit, the amount of work it did per "success," its costs per success, and so on.[2] The organization can then provide appropriate incentives to improve the performance of the laggards and reward the stars. Another meaning is the inclusion of the data system not only of measures of goal achievement but also of constraints that limit a program's capacity to meet its goals, both external and internal constraints such as budget cuts, failure of other agencies to cooperate, staff turnover. There is merit in this notion, but in a sense, it becomes a "don't-hold-me-accountability" system. However, the meaning that I will discuss is the accountability of the program to its publics and the ways that evaluation-oriented information systems can fulfill this function.

A program is responsible to different publics—to the funders, whether public or private, who provide the money; to its clients who are entitled to effective service; to other organizations, which refer clients, provide collateral services, or receive its departing successes or failures; to the general public. For the sake of illustration, let us look at the ways that an accountability system can be used to report to a community planning council or to an assembly of consumer groups.

The first essential—and this is a pretty novel idea as ideas go—is that at the outset, data have to be collected on the values and priorities of the intended audience: what objectives do they most value? On what basis will they judge the merit of the program? Are they concerned only with the achievement of the official goals of the program, or are they also interested in some of the political and symbolic functions that programs serve—degree of effort, style of service, visibility, community representation, etc. By finding out in advance the needs and priorities of the intended users of the data, the information system starts out with two advantages: (1) it knows what information is valued and therefore likely to be used, and (2) instead of adding more data on top, it can winnow out the unnecessary in advance and concentrate on priorities. An important reason for the history of neglect of even the most sophisticateed information outputs has been "data overload." Too much information is spewed out, more than decision-makers want, need, or can digest, and much of it is marginally relevant to their concerns. Here we start out with their own definitions of what is relevant.

Once the criteria of the audience are identified, measures of these criteria are developed and input into the system. Then at regular intervals, data are produced that display the success of the program on these measures. Since different publics are likely to have different values and priorities, the information system can become multidimensional and collect data that show "success" on the range of different criteria that are being applied. It may be that there are trade-offs among different criteria, that for example one of the planning council's criteria is inconsistent with a consumer group criterion: e.g., increased coverage of the target population may be inversely related to client satisfaction with services. Data, particularly the trend data over time that such a system produces, highlight such issues and may help lead to their resolution.

With the outcome data defined by the relevant publics, the accountabilty system allows periodic reporting of how well the program is doing in *their* terms. The outcome data can also be further analyzed, in much the manner of traditional evaluation research. Although this is not intrinsic to the notion of accountability, the system allows for analysis of program conditions that are associated with better or poorer perfor- mance on the criterion measures. It can indicate what the relationships are between outcomes and such factors as continuity of staffing, dollar expenditures, degree of citizen participation, or extended outreach activities. Because the information is regularly and systematically collected on a longtitudinal basis, it is possible to see the effects of program variations—both concurrent variations and variations over time. This provides sound bases for making decisions about program procedures.

The key characteristic of the accountability system is that it provides the information that the audience has defined as relevant to their values and their needs. It enables them to make decisions and take actions on the basis of the kind of information that they value.[3] It is important to keep the basic system as simple as possible so that the data clearly show what each audience wants to know. The system then provides incentives to improve the state of things. Each participating group (clients, managers, planners, funders) is encouraged to work for changes that will improve performance on the criteria that they have set, and each has ways of checking on the progress that is made.

These then are three of the possible models of program evaluation. Each is designed for different users facing different orders of decisions. The type of decision to be made—and the data that will help the decision-maker make that decision wisely—determine which model is appropriate.

One of the things an evaluator always asks of a program before undertaking a study is "What are the goals?" It is a question we less often ask about evaluation itself. But certainly if we had to answer the question, the primary answer would be that evaluation should make for better human services and wiser allocation of resources among and within programs. Only when we design evaluation to fit the needs of decision-makers—the issues they face, the information that will clarify the issues, and the salience to them of different kinds of information—do we stand a chance of reaching this goal.

Footnotes for Chapter 5

[1] Carol H. Weiss, "Evaluation Research in Political Context," paper prepared for presentation at the American Psychological Association meeting, Montreal, 1973.

[2] Robert A. Walker, "The Ninth Panacea: Program Evaluation," *Evaluation*, Vol. 1, No. 1 (1972), pp. 45-53.

[3] A. L. Service, S. J. Mantel, Jr., and A. Reisman, "Systems Analysis and Social Welfare Planning: A Case Study," in M. Mesarovic and A. Reisman (eds.), *Systems Approach and the City* (Amsterdam, Holland: North-Holland Publishing Co., 1973).

REFERENCE

Weiss, Carol H. *Evaluation Research: Methods of Assessing Program Effectiveness* (Englewood Cliffs, N.J.: Prentice-Hall, 1972).

COMMENTARY

Joseph W. Duncan

Dr. Weiss emphasizes an important, although infrequently made distinction, concerning analysis of the nature of evaluation itself. Just as the evaluator is concerned with (1) defining program goals, (2) developing measures or indicators of goal achievement, (3) analyzing and comparing program participants with appropriate control groups, and (4) drawing conclusions, it is appropriate to consider the same approach when reviewing the usefulness of different evaluation techniques.

The three basic models which Dr. Weiss has labeled "social experimentation", "traditional evaluation", and "accountability" highlight the distinctions in goals among various types of evaluation systems.

It is frequently pointed out that social experimentation must take proper account of the environment of the experiment itself. The experiment in the social laboratory (the real world) is taking place under conditions which are continually changing and which are beyond the control of those responsible for the experiment.

At Battelle, our social scientists have been engaged in two major social experiments where these issues have become important. They are:

1. A project for the Office of Economic Opportunity directed to elucidation of the performance/incentive relation in remedial education.[1]

2. Companion projects sponsored by the Department of Health, Education and Welfare and by the Law Enforcement Assistance Administration to study (1) alternatives to incarceration and (2) rehabilitation of Federal offenders.[2]

Through review of data gathered from various social experiments two statisticians, Dr. Ralph E. Thomas of Battelle's Columbus Laboratories and Dr. Carl A. Bennett of the Human Affairs Research Center, have been developing insights into the characterization of those social questions that can be pursued by means of large-scale social experiments and defining relevant methodologies. Their research suggests that some of the characteristics of an appropriate methodology are:[3]

1. It must attempt to determine the objective content of data in the presence of inherent biases due to collection and selection.
2. It must recognize the dynamic nature of social data, both in terms of the fleeting and perishable nature of attitudes and opinions and the constantly changing nature of human value structures, and hence social priorities.
3. It must seek solutions that are feasible and robust, rather than optimal. The best today cannot be the best tomorrow; what is optimal for one location or environment will not be optimal for another. Rather than strive to optimize, we need to learn how to select those solutions that are widely applicable in both space and time, and hence generally and lastingly acceptable."

The last item concerning "robustness" is of particular importance in the perspective of Dr. Weiss' paper since it suggests that much of the conflict between "scientific approaches to social problems" and "the political processes" may simply reflect the basic difference in analytical approach between the scientific optimal and the robust (politically acceptable) solution. Recognition of these differences is, of course, difficult in specific situations. For example, while the social scientist is typically associated with analysis of the social implications of actions, it is not uncommon for the politicians to be more concerned than the social scientist with the problem of broad public acceptability of a solution since the politician is looking forward to reelection and, hence, holds a specifically defined concept of public acceptability. Likewise, while the politician is frequently accused of short-term interest, there are occasions when a social scientist, seeking the acclaim of his peer group, may urge short-range approaches to gain attention to the ideas being proposed. In any case, the distinction between scientific optimal and politically acceptable is at the core of much of the debate concerning the effectiveness of evaluation.

In the context of these realities it is surprising that Dr. Weiss takes the following position with respect to social experimentation. She states, "Since they (the social experimenters) are dealing with true experiments, there is little uncertainty about whether it is the program or extraneous conditions that are causing the observed effects. Since the program adheres to well-defined principles and procedures, there is little uncertainty about whether the program has had a fair test or whether its failings are the result of faulty administration or operation. Since variants of the basic program are operated, there is information about the sets of conditions that have greater or lesser payoff."

In contrast to this set of quotations I would suggest that the uncertainties associated with social experimentation are even greater than those identified with traditional evaluation approaches (even when one accounts for the ex-post character of many traditional evaluation studies). For example, in the evaluation of income maintenance programs the test results concerning the disincentives may prove to be misleading. Implementation of income maintenance programs on a full-scale basis, with attendant publicity and public education may lead to a totally different set of results from the specific incentives or program variants observed during the social experiment.[4]

This difficulty may be labeled "Problems of Scale Effects". In mechanical engineering problems of scale are frequently important. For example, in fluid dynamics the aerodynamic characteristics of a model in the wind tunnel may be quite different from the full-scale patterns in actual flight conditions. A similar set of "scale effects" is associated with social experimentation as we move from the pilot effort to the full implementation of a social program. Hence, I submit the uncertainties of social experimention are greater than suggested by Dr. Weiss in her paper.

In closing, I would like to add emphasis to one of the clients of evaluation research—the consumer of the social services which are being evaluated. Dr. Weiss appropriatelydrew attention to the intended audience of the evaluation study (a point which is echoed in Higgs' paper)—namely, the decision-maker in the program agency. I would like to extend that concept of intended audience to include the clients of the agency[5] to assure that indicators of program effectiveness are specifically related to the concerns and experiences of those receiving the service. Time and time again it has been demonstrated that single-purpose agencies—while effective in their speciality—are often ineffective in the community-at-large because of difficulties associated with intake and qualification, with inappropriate diagnosis, and with infrastructure problems such as transportation accessibility. Provided that the agency decision-maker is acceptable to the idea of responding to perceived needs in the community, the involvement of structured "consumer analysis" can help assure that the evaluator's effort will be beneficial to both the general public and to the sponsoring agency. The addition of data concerning the expectations or objectives of the client to data concerning characteristics of the client can be obtained with a minimally additional effort. The consequence, however, can be most significant by adding the force of effective client service to effective decision-making within the agency to assure a higher quality of outcome for the human service program.

Footnotes for Commentary

[1] Battelle's Columbus Laboratories, "Test and Analysis Services for a Performance-Incentive Remedial Education Experiment," Office of Economic Opportunity, 1971.

[2] Battelle Human Affairs Research Center (Seattle), "Assessment of Alternatives to Incarceration," Law Enforcement Assistance Administration, 1972, and "Federal Offenders Rehabilitation Program," Division of Vocational Rehabilitation, State of Washington.

[3] A more lengthy discussion of these points is found in Research Futures, First Quarter 1973, published by Memorial Institute, Office of Corporate Communications, Columbus, Ohio, 1973,

[4] For discussion of further difficulties see Edgar K. Browning, "Incentive and Disincentive Experimentation for Income Maintenance Policy Purposes," the *American Economic Review*, September, 1971, p. 709. "The results of such an experiment cannot be generalized to provide reliable information concerning the disincentive effects of an income maintenance policy. The reason is that the aggregate market effects of such a policy will not occur in the sample study, and cannot be inferred from the experimental results...''The sample will always be a negligible part of the entire market, so that there will be no noticiable pressure on the market wage rates change." (p. 710).

[5] Dr. Weiss briefly mentioned an assembly of client groups as a potential audience for the evaluation report; an implicit recognition of the clients as a potential audience for evaluation research.

PART III

PROFILES ON PROGRAM EVALUATION

CHAPTER 6

Evaluating Integrated Service Programs:
A Case Study of The East Cleveland Project

R. O. Washington
John B. Turner

There is a general feeling among human services program designers and policy analysts as well as the day-to-day administrators of human services programs that the evaluation indices commonly used to measure the general well-being of our society fall short of adequacy in terms of precision and reliability. GNP measures only market transactions. It tells us almost nothing about the social well-being of the general population in terms of (1) health and illness; (2) social mobility; (3) the adequacy of the physical environment; (4) individual income and poverty; (5) public order and safety; (6) the promotion of science and art and the equality of educational opportunities; or (7) participation and alienation. As the report of the National Commission on Technology, Automation, and Economic Progress[1] pointed out, a GNP ". . . tells us little about pockets of poverty, depressed communities, sick industries, etc."

The inadequacy of existing indices and measures prompted the Commission to recommend a "system of social accounts" aimed at bringing about, through new concepts and measures, what it judged to be a much needed new framework. This new framework would ". . . give us a broader and more balanced reckoning of the meaning of social and economic progress . . . and move us toward measurement of the utilization of human resources . . ." in terms of social costs and net returns of economic innovations; reduction and amelioration of social ills (e.g., crime, family disruption); the creation of "performance budgets" in areas of defined social needs (e.g., housing, education); and economic opportunity and social mobility.

The Commission hoped that, eventually, such a framework would provide a "balance sheet" which could be used to clarify policy choices.

Shortly after the widespread distribution of that report, the Secretary of Health, Education and Welfare, John W. Gardner, at the direction of President Johnson, appointed a panel of social scientists to advise the government on the development of "social indicators" to measure social change and to help with the possible preparation of a social report comparable to the Economic Report rendered annually by the President's Council of Economic Advisors. The product of that effort, entitled Toward a Social Report, was submitted to the President in early 1969. The report identified the seven aforementioned policy areas from which social indicators could be drawn to measure social well-being. The Panel felt that the collection of new socially relevant data in each of the major social policy areas would provide a balanced, organized and concise set of measures of the conditions of society. It was hoped that such data would also generate information needed to identify emerging social problems, to plan effective solutions, and to make knowledgeable policy-related decisions about the efficiency, effectiveness, and performance of programs designed to implement these policy decisions.

Research in the field of social accounting has made a great deal of progress since 1969. However, there are still unfilled interspaces of knowledge, in terms of conceptual clarity and methodological preciseness. These gaps exist, according to the editors of this volume, because of certain institutional and human predicaments which are not given sufficient consideration. One of these they described as the difficulty in defining social problems and hence the goals of social programs.

The general aim of this chapter shall be to examine this predicament and to present illustrative data regarding how a suburban community—East Cleveland, Ohio—grappled with it. We shall describe how the community conceived and developed an integrated services program which included procedures for insuring accountability of service delivery.

Conditions That Gave Rise To ECCHSC

The City of East Cleveland is a suburban community situated in the northeastern portion of the State of Ohio. It lies northeast of downtown Cleveland and is bounded on the east and south by a prosperous suburban community which, in turn, limits East Cleveland's opportunity for industrial growth and expansion. At the turn of the century, East Cleveland was a wealthy village of 3,985 people. However, the next two decades saw major growth both in population and in the physical development of the city. In 1920, the population of East Cleveland was 27,292, and 49.5% of the present housing stock had been built. Moreover, by 1910, approximately 15% of the population was foreign-born white and 85% native-born white. These proportions remained constant with minor fluctuations until the 1960's.

In the 1960's, East Cleveland shifted rapidly from an all-white to a biracial city. In 1960, blacks constituted 2.4% of the population, but in 1967, a professional survey showed that nearly half of the population—44.6%—was black. Today, it is estimated that 70% (28,000) of the population is black.

One of the most important factors accounting for this in-migration was the availability of better housing close to Cleveland at a price which blacks could afford. For many blacks, as for many foreign-born whites earlier in the century, East Cleveland provided their first opportunity to become homeowners. A second important factor was East Cleveland's reputation for good city services: police, schools, fire, sanitation.

A third factor to attract blacks to East Cleveland was the apparent efficiency of city government. Since 1918, East Cleveland has had a City Manager and City Commission with a stable, good-government tradition. The five City Commissioners are elected every four years; the elections are non-partisan and usually non-controversial. The President of the Commission is also by charter the Mayor of the City. The City Commissioners appoint the City Manager, and he holds office at their discretion. By charter, the City Commissioners are legislators and set policy, while the City Manager is responsible for the administration of the city government. The City Manager appoints all department heads and carries out policy set by the City Commission.

The black in-migration shifted the population from middle-age families to young families with small children. The population under 24 years of age expanded from 33.7% of the population in 1960 to close to 50% by 1973.

There was also an increase in the number of laborers and operatives, however, and municipal revenues increased very little. A recent breakdown by occupations showed that whites in lower-middle income occupations were moving out and being replaced primarily by blacks in semi-skilled and un-skilled occupations, with a small elite of black professionals. On the other hand, the older white population did not leave the city at the same rate as did the white middle-age and young families.

By 1973, there was a dramatic increase in the number of welfare recipients in the percentage of children in East Cleveland schools from welfare families. Since January 1969, the number of individuals receiving some type of public assistance has increased over 400%. The percentage of students enrolled in the East Cleveland public schools receiving public assistance has increased over 1,500% since 1965, from 206 to 3,327.

Thus, between 1960 and 1970 the tax base and public income declined with younger, lower-income, dependent or unemployed persons replacing middle-age and higher income persons. At the same time, there was a sharply increased need for municipal and educational services to schoolage-children, young adults, breadwinners close to the poverty line, welfare recipients below it, and older people.

The level of municipal and educational services a community can provide, and the degree to which the community resources can be mobilized for the enrichment of the lives of its residents are determined in no small measure by that community's tax base and the public income. In inner-ring suburbs across the country, the influx of poorer black population and the squeeze between demand for services and declining municipal revenues have been precursors of block-busting realtors, abandonment by white middle-class leadership and economic interests, and the rapid deterioration of an impoverished community into yet another ghetto. This fate East Cleveland city government was determined to avoid.

In 1967, with a city commission of two black and three white members, the city fathers realized their efforts were not enough. A more planned and coordinated approach was needed to preserve the community from socio-economic decline. The city commission, with the support of community leaders, decided upon certain directions the city should take. With the help of a grant from Housing and Urban Development (HUD), the commission established a community renewal program. The Community Renewal Program (CRP) had several components; one of these provided for a professional survey of the city's physical structure and citizen attitudes, which was to be the basis for a program of community development.

The survey report, which was published two years later, called for economic development activities, commercial and industrial development, and increased human services to the residents. Following the release of the survey report, a series of meetings and deliberations among City Commissioners were held; out of these emerged the idea for a comprehensive social services delivery system. The East Cleveland Community Human Services Center is the product of that enterprise.

The East Cleveland Community Human Services Center (ECCHSC)

In order that the reader may fully understand the strategy for insuring accountability of integrated services delivery, perhaps a brief discussion of the concept of services integration as well as the political ethos which gave rise to the project is warranted.

Services Integration. It is difficult, if perhaps not impossible, to pinpoint the source and genesis of the concept of services integration. As a matter of fact, it has been referred to as ". . . an evolving art about which little is known."[2] It is perhaps fair to say, however, that the concept responds to deliberate efforts at welfare reform at both the national and local levels of social planning.

The thrusts of services integration are the prevention and reduction of economic dependency and more effective organization, coordination and administration of social services. The concept of services integration has developed in response to a fragmented pattern of service delivery in which separate programs are developed without consideration given to the multiple service needs of their clientele. What is more, certain programs tend to serve separate clientele.

Translated in terms of local service delivery, the goal of services integration is the development of a strategy for assessing the total human services needs of an entire family at a single location with a single application; and, then providing such services ". . . constrained only by the state of the art and the availability of resources."[3]

HEW Secretary Elliott Richardson in a memorandum in 1971 set forth the requisites of an integrated services framework:

The coordinated delivery of services for the greatest benefit to people.
A holistic approach to the individual and family unit.

The provision of a comprehensive range of services locally.
The rational allocation of resources at the local level so as to be responsive to local needs.

The East Cleveland services integration project, called the East Cleveland Community Human Services Center (ECCHSC), was conceived and developed over several years of deliberation and planning. The center responds to a community need for improved and expanded social services as well as a new and more effective service delivery mode. A significant element of this services integration project is the participation of a general purpose government, the City of East Cleveland, as the services integrator. Traditionally, the entire chain of social services in a community has not been seen as a single system; linkage and integration have been haphazard and loose. Consumers move into and out of the jurisdiction of these separate service agencies with no one attending to transitions and hiatuses or accepting responsibility for the workings of the system as a whole.

Services integration under the sponsorship of a general purpose government takes on the character of a *community system* in which programs and services are meshed by local leadership. To the extent that a general purpose government can serve as a funding conduit, develop administrative linkages among service agencies, facilitate social service capacity building within the community, assist in establishing priorities for social service planning, and provide for mechanisms of accountability of service delivery, it becomes an important facilitator of services integration. One general objective of the evaluation, then, was to measure the extent to which a general purpose government is better able to sponsor effective services integration than are other organizational auspices.

Another innovative feature of this project was the formulation and development of a *case management* approach to service delivery. Case management incorporates the idea of management-by-objectives. Conceptually, case management is a consumer-centered, goal-oriented strategy for social service delivery. This mode of service delivery is aimed ultimately at assisting the consumer to become self-sufficient. It begins from the premise that the goals of the consumer are the goals of the Case Manager. To this extent, the Case Manager becomes the advocate of the consumer in furthering the latter's needs. Drawing upon his own expertise, the Case Manager seeks first to understand the consumer's goal and his perception of reality and helps the consumer to perceive his goal in an objectively realistic manner. He then selects those goals which appear attainable, given the state-of-the-art and the availability of resources and influence.

The Case Manager serves as the key person for "orchestrating" services required to help the consumer to move toward self-support or self-care. His key role is services integration, through brokerage and advocacy activities, and is focused upon the meshing of simultaneous or sequential services and interventions and negotiating on behalf of the consumer to insure access and continuity. He conducts follow-up to see that the service was delivered and attempts to ascertain from the consumer his utilization of and satisfaction with the services.

Formulating An Evaluation Strategy

It is the position of these authors that human services programs which emphasize services integration require an evaluation strategy which is "formative" in character. That is, evaluation should be ongoing with provisions for regular feedback to the Project Administrator so that program modifications can be made while the program is still fluid.

Program Administrators will need to weigh the pros and cons of inside versus outside evaluation in light of their own administrative styles. In the case of the East Cleveland project, the Program Administrator attempted to achieve the best of both worlds (i.e., the objectivity and autonomy of an outside evaluator and the intimate knowledge about program goals of an inside evaluator) by hiring the services of a research organization from a nearby university. Under a third party contract between the Project and the university, a Research and Evaluation Department was integrated into the project. While the Research and Evaluation Department enjoyed the amenities of a consultant group, it had all the advantages of an "in-house" operation.

Another factor of major importance is that the Research and Evaluation Department was a part of the organizational structure from the very inception of the program. Therefore, the evaluation strategy for measuring program performance was conceived simultaneously with the formulation of program goals. The Evaluators developed an evaluation paradigm which consisted of an eight-step sequence which formed what was called a behavioral model of evaluation (BME). A description of this step-by-step sequence of activities follows.

Specifying Goals. As Figure 1 shows, integrated services programs have two sets of goals. The first set is systematic goals established by federal policy and guidelines. They constitute one group of parameters within which all federally supported social service activities are conducted. There are four basic systemic goals which have been established by HEW. They are:

To provide supportive services to assist individuals in preparing for, obtaining, and holding gainful employment.

To assist aged, blind, and disabled adults to manage their own affairs and maintain independence, and to provide protection when they can no longer manage their own affairs independently.

To strengthen and improve family living, promote family stability, and prevent or alleviate family dysfunction.

To provide services to or in behalf of children and youth in public assistance or other low-income families and to neglected, abused, and homeless children of all economic levels in order to protect them and to foster their normal growth and development.

The second set of goals are service goals which in our case are defined by: (1) the expectations of the City of East Cleveland, as the project sponsor, and (2) the needs of consumers. The Evaluators must therefore be concerned with both sets of goals. As participants in program planning and development, they lend their expert knowledge in helping the Program Administrator to determine which of the systemic goals the project ought to pursue. Such factors as organizational clout, political ethos, and financial resources will govern this decision.

The Evaluators are concerned with local service goals because they become: (1) the other parameters within which the project operates, which are maximized by moving people from some level of dependency toward self-care, and (2) the basis for establishing accountability of service delivery. In this sense, a formative evaluation strategy serves as the axis around which the service delivery system maintains quality control.

Since the evaluation strategy of the East Cleveland Project emphasized a behavioral approach, a clear definition of service goals and objectives was essential. The Evaluators began from the premise that service goals are derived from a statement of consumer needs. A need is defined as a problem that exists because of discrepancy which can be seen between the ideal state of a variable and its actual state. That is, the agency and the Evaluators postulate a desirable value for a variable such as education, health, employment status, etc., and a problem is then defined as the discrepancy between the desirable and the actual condition for a given consumer. Once needs are specified in terms of discrepancies, service objectives can be formulated by postulating a reduction of need (discrepancy) with a temporal context.

Four methods were used for documenting human needs and social problems. Before any goals were agreed upon, the project, in conjunction with the city's CRP, hired a consultant firm to conduct a community survey, part of which involved a human needs assessment. Once the project had determined which of the systemic goals it would pursue, a 3% household survey was conducted. This second procedure was considered necessary because of the need to have a standardized unit of data collection such as the household. The household was considered a key element because it represents the smallest social unit of communication, social control, power distribution, and socialization readily accessible. Within it, income is distributed, housing is shared, and children are reared.[4]

Codification of unmet needs based upon day-to-day service requests constituted the third technique. A fourth attempt to document unmet needs involved the establishment of an "adequacy of performance" index in which data about the lack of contact with existing appropriate services, lack of an appropriate service, and lack of utilization of existing services was computed against "universe of needs" data collected through the community survey. This technique is a highly empirical approach and is likely to be more useful as a planning device than as a measurement tool.

The formulation of service goals and objectives should

Figure 1
Integrated Services Projects Goal Structure

SYSTEMIC GOALS

Systemic goals are set by Federal policy and represent national goals. They relate to the expressed intent of certain federal legislations and services mandated by these legislations.

$\downarrow$

SERVICE GOALS

Service goals are organizational goals selected by the Services Integration Project, These goals should derive from empirically established needs in the local community and should reflect the committment and capacity of all agencies and services which constitute the integrated services delivery system.
Service goals may be identical to systemic goals in certain projects, depending upon defined needs and the availability of resources.

$\downarrow$

CONSUMER GOALS

Consumer goals are subsumed under service goals. They relate to the specific needs and requests of consumers and are stated in terms of the behavior the consumer should display at the end of the service episode.

$\downarrow$

SERVICE OBJECTIVES

Service objectives are statements which define the steps to be taken with individual consumers in order to produce the changes implied by the goal. Service objectives constitute criterion tasks; when they are completed, the consumer goal is considered to have been achieved.

include a statement of the actual changes in the problem the service system will attempt to produce; such statements are frequently referred to as descriptions of outcomes. The objectives, on the other hand, should state specific steps that must be taken with each consumer in order to produce the changes implied by the goal. When all the objectives have been met, the goal is considered to have been achieved.

This reasoning is particularly important in measuring the effectiveness of a project like East Cleveland. For example, when a resident comes in for service, he is referred to a Case Manager. The Case Manager must explore with the consumer his problem and then agree upon some particular goal. The Case Manager then prepares a service plan which the consumer approves. This plan when signed by both parties becomes a service contract.

From the Evaluators' perspective, the service contract must be written so that the goal is stated in behavioral terms. The service contract must also specify what actions both the consumer and the Case Manager must take. These criterion tasks become the objectives. Viewed in the context of goal-oriented social services (GOSS), these criterion tasks represent the establishment of conditions necessary for the achievement of the goal. Each time a task is completed, a barrier to the achievement of the goal has been removed.

It becomes clear, then, that an efficient strategy for achieving accountability of service delivery must begin with a clear definition of both systemic and service goals. One of the initial ways in which the Evaluators provide valuable technical assistance to the Program Administrator, then, is to help him clearly define these goals in terms of outcomes. As a matter of fact, for programs which are in their capacity-building stage, the thrust of the evaluation effort during this period may very well center around the determination of whether the goals and objectives are clearly defined.

Specification Of Evaluation Objectives. Specifying goals as discussed in the preceding section is as much a planning and program development process as it is an evaluation task. Formulating evaluation objectives, on the other hand, is viewed solely as a part of the evaluation strategy.

Evaluation objectives provide the Evaluators with an analytical famework within which to conduct the evaluation. Since this evaluation strategy calls for the Evaluators to be an integral part of the organization from the outset, evaluation objectives should be prepared simultaneously with service goals. They should flow logically from service goals and should aim to measure or assess the outcome behavior in light of service goals. They should be stated in such a way as to infer the "causal" relationship between the program intervention (the independent variable) and some desired effect (the dependent variable).

Evaluation objectives are more than statements of the purpose of the evaluation; they bring closure around the evaluation tasks by specifying quantitative measures and specifying the criterion condition accepted as a standard of program success. Measurements and other evaluation activities should focus upon the determination of whether or not the criterion has been met. Each evaluation objective should specify the targets for change and the amount of change required to meet the social change outcome criterion.

Targets for change* may be classified as: (1) persons or groups who are regarded as either deviants or problem individuals, or persons affected by problem individuals, or persons who are objects of undesirable activities or conditions; (2) professionals or other individuals who are functionaries of service delivery systems; (3) physical objects or territorial units such as housing conditions, recreational facilities, or neighborhoods. It should be pointed out that the outcomes of program interventions upon targets for change are not necessarily dependent variables. They may represent "means" changes; and are "ends" changes only insofar as they represent changes in the behavior of members of the consumer group. For example, the increase in expenditures for social service programs, the changes in the ratio of case managers to consumers, or of physicians or policemen per population may occur in the process of service delivery. However, program outcomes should be measured only in terms of reduction in dependency, improved health, and reduction in crime rates, respectively.

*We are indebted to Dr. Howard Freeman and the Russell Sage Foundation for this concept; however, we assume responsibility for the interpretation used here.

In addition to specifying the amount of change required, the evaluation objectives should also specify how many subjects within the sample must attain the criterion condition in order for the program to be declared a success in regard to a particular service goal.

Specification Of Dependent Variables (Social Change Outcome Criteria). The perspective within which dependent variables are defined is couched in the behavioral construct. We begin from the premise that behavior may be defined in terms of some function of an environmental stimulus; therefore, one effective way of changing behavior is by changing the environmental circumstances which influence it. The dependent variable with which the Evaluators deal, then, is behavior, and the independent variables which control behavior are elements of the environment. Also important in this paradigm is the notion that all behavior conforms to causal laws. It is neither random nor capricious, but orderly with discoverable uniformities.

As was pointed out earlier, the dependent variable for most program activities in the East Cleveland Project was defined in terms of behavior (performance) which the consumer was expected to be able to demonstrate as evidence that the consumer goal had been met. The principle employed was that the dependent variable should be specified in such a way as to allow the outcome of the program to be measured in terms of the competence of the consumer to negotiate or gain mastery over his social environment. Indices of mastery over the environment are measures of changes from one level of dependency to a higher level of independence or evidence of improved life chances. Gil defined these as ". . . changes in the quality of life or the level of well-being of society's members, as observed on demographic, biological, psychological, social, economic, political, cultural and ecological indicators."[5] Specifically, he defined indices of mastery over the environment as:

Changes in the development of life-sustaining and life-enhancing resources, goods and services.
Changes in the allocation to individuals and social units of specific statuses.
Changes in the distribution to individuals and social units of rights and rights equivalents.

Changes in rewards, entitlements, and constraints, and in the proportion of rights distributed as rewards and entitlements.
Changes in the quality and quantity of real and symbolic resources, goods and services distributed.
Changes in the proportion of rights throughout society and in the degree of structural inequality of rights among individual members and social units.
Changes in the extent of coverage of a defined level of minimum rights for all members of society.
Changes in the extent to which the distribution of rights is linked to allocation of statuses.

Using this frame of reference made it easy for Case Managers to prepare service plans because service goals are selected on the basis of the social problems and the needs of the consumer at the time that the program intervention is planned.

Using the behavioral principle of causality along with empirical data collected about the outcomes of antecedent interventions, the Case Manager is then able to select certain program objectives (criterion tasks) that will lead to a specific problem solution or amelioration. Furthermore, since the Case Manager and the consumer must agree upon the service plan, both are clear and in agreement about what evidence will be used to measure the effectiveness of service delivery. The significance of this circumstance from a policy point of view relates to the proposition that the consumer has a right to help decide his own fate, and, in turn, has a right to make some judgment about the extent to which the service system is effective in providing for his needs and indirectly for the needs of the larger community.

What this means in terms of an evaluation strategy is that data derived from outcome evaluation, client-satisfaction surveys, etc., must be codified in such a way as to provide Case Managers with a capacity to make certain predictions about certain service objectives—provided they have sufficient demographic information about the consumer. In terms of system accountability, what this means is that the Evaluators must set up a data collection mechanism which collects the kind of evidence they need to measure program effectiveness and which at the same time is useful in the reformulation of service objectives. Such a strategy must be integrated into the program in such a way as to put program planning, development, and evaluation into a circular form that systematically contributes to rational decision-making.

Verification Of Independent Variables. Along with the identification of outcome criteria, the Evaluators must incorporate into the evaluation design various measures of input, which logically constitute measures of the independent (cause) variables or program intervention.

Welty defined independent variables as "input variables,"[6] i.e., a set of dimensions of behavior that exists upon the subject's entry into the program, and that will be changed by the action of the program.

This phase of the evaluation is process-oriented. That is, focus is upon identifying those processes by which the program operates. The task of the Evaluators is to identify and isolate elements of interaction and interrelations which verify the existence of a relationship between program activities and outcomes. Suchman suggested that this process involves raising two major questions: *What* is producing the desired change? *Why* is this change coming about?[7] We contend that a more basic question to be raised during this phase of the evaluation is: *Did* any change occur and what is the significance of the change in terms of magnitude and temporal dimensions. In other words, is it a change in an amount that is of any consequence at a particular point in time.

Earlier, we gave an example of a type of "means" change. Another way to look at the notion of "means" changes is to relate it to changes that occur in the behavior of the project staff, other service providers, and members of the granting organization in the process of service delivery. This idea is supported by the proposition that all living organisms engage in a complex interchange with their respective environment, in the course of which they modify and are modified by what they encounter. Whether one treats these changes as independent or intervening variables depends largely upon the analytical framework within which the evaluation is conducted.

Specification Of Intervening Variables. Intervening variables are defined as a set of functional processes that interconnect and mediate between the initiating causes of behavior, on the one hand, and the final resulting behavior, on the other. Suchman suggested that the purpose of isolating intervening variables is (1) to test the "spuriousness" of one's attribution of effectiveness to the intervention, (2) to elaborate upon conditions which modify the effectiveness of the program, and (3) to specify the process whereby the program leads to the desired effect.[8]

Intervening variable analysis in evaluative research also assists the evaluator in determining what factors had a debilitating effect upon the program. Bateman, looking at training programs, identified four such variables. These are: (1) the location of the project; (2) the characteristics of the trainees served; (3) the availability of services in relation to requirements; and (4) the skills with which these services are organized to accomplish the mission. He observed:

> . . . Other things being equal, training projects operating in areas of high unemployment would be expected to be less successful than those operating in areas where labor markets are tight. Similarly, projects in which participants have a lower average level of educational attainment and a higher average age and in which there is a higher proportion of female and non-white participants will probably be less successful in ultimately achieving the objective of assuring greater earnings for its trainees. . . . Similarly, projects in areas where resources for basic education and training are scarce and day care or similar facilities are unavailable will be hard pressed to produce results comparable to other projects serving essentially the same types of trainees and facing similar labor market conditions but with adequate resources and facilities. Finally, differences in the abilities of project managers are crucial in accounting for differences in project effectiveness.[9]

In the East Cleveland Project we found another variable which affects the relative success of a project. That is, the community image of the project held by the population to be served by the project. Although our project was designed to serve all citizens of the community, it was constantly fighting the image of a "welfare project." Such an image during the early development of the project had a strong debilitating impact upon outreach efforts to non-welfare residents.

Data Collection. As noted earlier, an evaluation strategy such as the one employed at the East Cleveland Project requires a highly developed client information and retrieval system. As pointed out earlier, since service goals derive from a universe of need, one measure of program effectiveness is a reduction of needs over time. This meant that the project was required to maintain accurate records regarding the demographic characterists of consumers, and their needs, service plans, and contracts and follow-up information about client satisfaction.

Any evaluation design seeks to answer questions related to at least the following: (a) *Effectiveness*—Did any change occur? Was the change the one intended? Here emphasis is upon measuring results. (b) *Significance*—Here, concern is upon impact and the meaningfulness of the outcome. It relates to such questions as: Will the achievement of the goals contribute to the economic development or social well-being of the people served? Does the achievement of service goals contribute to the accomplishment of the stated systemic goals, and to what extent? Are goals soundly conceived or appropriate in terms of needs? What are the program's advantages over possible alternatives? And what are the "spillover" effects? (c) *Efficiency*—This is concerned with the question: Is the cost reasonable and do the benefits justify the costs?

These three criteria may be applied to both systemic and service goals and serve to define the type of evidence to be collected for judging program performance. Such criteria of success, then, aid the evaluator in identifying indices of the dependent variable.

One of the unique features of the data collection process used in this project was to relate evidence of effectiveness to regions of effect. The notion of regions of effect was originally developed by Hyman, Wright, and Hopkins.[10] As expanded upon here, a region of effect is the intended general social problem area to be treated by the program intervention. It aids in determining both the kinds of evidence required for measuring effecteve service delivery and the type of data which matches best with the predetermined outcome. For example, when we evaluated the manpower component of the project, the designated region of effect was economic dependency. In this case, we attempted to collect as evidence of effect changes in rates of unemployment, and the state of dependency of the target population, reduction in transfer payments by the government, etc. On the other hand, we were concerned with the quality of the training, attitudes of instructors, accessibility of the training site, etc., only insofar as these factors were treated as independent or intervening variables.

It should perhaps be pointed out here that since our evaluation strategy relied heavily upon behavioral science research methods, we used questonnaires, attitude scales, and interviews as the primary bases of data collection. It is our belief that when these instruments have been constructed with appropriate care, i.e., have been developed to guard against problems of internal and external validity, and are selected to address that which they are designed to measure, then such instruments are valid and reliable tools.

Data Analysis. As alluded to earlier in the chapter, every evaluation design must have an analytical framework within which the evaluation will be conducted. The major focus of our evaluation strategy was to measure program effectiveness in terms of helping consumers to gain mastery over their respective environments and to measure accountability of service delivery. The analytical framework for the East Cleveland Project was derived from the behavioral paradigm and open-systems theory. We have already presented a brief discussion of the application of behavioral concepts to our evaluation strategy.

The open-systems framework used by this project was originally developed by Leonard Goodwin. According to Goodwin, a governmental social service delivery system consists of three subsystems.[11]

The first, as depicted in Figure 2, is that of the donor subsystem. At the federal level, it includes congressmen, the administration and federal agencies who make laws, allocate funds, and develop guidelines and mandates for the implementation of federal social service programs. At the local level, in the case of East Cleveland, it also included the City Commissioners who passed certain legislations which governed the administration of the project as well as the allocation of certain funds.

At the other end of the figure is the consumer subsystem which represents the target population. The circular figure that intersects and joins together the donor and consumer subsystems is the service delivery subsystem. It includes program staff, site and facilities, and a mode of intervention.

The interaction of members from these three subsystems is indicated by the crosshatched overlap of the figures. These crosshatched areas represent interfaces. Members of the service delivery subsystem interact with members of the donor subsystem in Interface 1, and with members of the consumer subsystem in Interface 2.

Figure 2
Elements of an Integrated Services Program

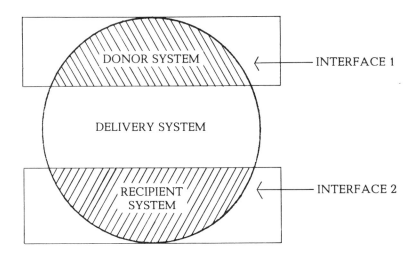

Expanding upon Goodwin's model and applying it to program evaluation, the task of the behaviorally oriented Evaluators then is to determine the quality of the two interfaces. This is measured in terms of: (1) the extent to which the delivery subsystem helps members of the consumer subsystem to gain mastery over their respective environments as depicted by Interface 2, and (2) the extent to which the service delivery subsystem facilitates accountability between the donor subsystem and consumer subsystem displayed in Interface 1. As pointed out earlier, mastery over the environment is measured in terms of changes in levels of dependency and improved life chances and may represent any one of the changes described by Gil. (See section on dependent variables.)

Accountability of service delivery is measured in terms of responsiveness to consumer needs. Responsiveness to consumer needs relates to the *availability* of services and the *efficiency* in the delivery of services. Kaplan et al. suggested that the availability of service can be examined from two dimensions:

(1) accessibility—the ease with which the consumer is able to enter the system, and (2) continuity—the ease with which the consumer is able to move within the system. Efficiency in the delivery of services is measured in terms of reduction of costs and of duplication of service delivery, and in terms of economies of scale.[12]

Using this line of thinking, then, one index of mastery over the environment was the change in the behavior of the consumer from the point of entry into the social service system to the point of exit. Also, quality of services was treated as either independent or intervening variables, depending upon data empirically developed during the course of analysis. Quality of service relates to the organizational structure; nature, frequency and length of services; nature of technology used; characteristics and qualifications of personnel providing services; characteristics of consumers, including their value orientations in terms of self, as well as their expectations regarding services and interventions.

Feedback. As we have already described, our evaluation design emphasized a formative strategy. That is, it was designed to provide feedback information to the Program Administrator and the staff at any time during program implementation. Feedback data were used to modify program operations and to make and changes which seemed to foster the achievement of program outcomes.

Since the Evaluators are integral members of the project staff, they can provide client satisfaction information to Case Managers and other members of the staff shortly after the completion of each episode of service. Inasmuch as client satisfaction is measured in terms of satisfaction with the process as well as with outcomes, the Evaluators also provide information to members of the entire delivery system about the services integration process—particularly with respect to assessibility and continuity. Furthermore, because the Evaluators have the responsibility for providing needs assessment data and determining whether service goals and priorities conform to needs data, they can provide authoritative data for program modification.

Our total evaluation strategy relied heavily upon the analysis of data derived from "before and after" measurements, in which assessments of the status of the consumer before service or intervention provided baseline data, and after intervention, provided outcome data. The advantage of such an evaluation system is that the outcome data from one set of service delivery activities become the baseline data (input) for the set of modified activities.

This cybernetic approach in which outcome data are treated as input within some temporal dimension is a key element of the feedback process. In other words, the feedback process is the nexus between service delivery and accountability. It serves as the communication network which produces action (alternative intervention strategies) among Case Managers in response to an input of information, and at the same time includes the results of previous actions in the new information which is provided to them for meeting subsequent goals.

For example, when the Evaluators conduct a follow-up on a service agreement, they determine the extent to which the agreed-upon criterion tasks contributed to the achievement of the service goal specified in the service agreement. They examine both independent and intervening variables which operated during the intervention process and provides information about their effectiveness, significance, and efficiency of program activities.

If the feedback is well designed, including information about demographic characteristics of consumers, temporal aspects of service outcomes, identification of unanticipated consequences, etc., the result will be the accumulation of a "bank" of criterion tasks which the Case Manager will be able to draw from in pursuing certain service goals, depending upon the demographic characteristics of the consumer.

A well designed feedback process must be incorporated as a part of the evaluation system at the outset of program development. It is, therefore, essential that the Program Administrator establish an official channel through which feedback data is provided. In the case of the East Cleveland Project, there were two vehicles. The Evaluators were able to present formative data at the weekly administrative staff meetings which included the Program Administrator and supervisors.

If the Evaluators wished to make recommendations which involved major changes which affected policy or new areas of service delivery, such recommendations were made in the form of what was called a Program Action Proposal (PAP). The purpose of a program action proposal was to (1) specify the universe of need on a particular social problem variable, (2) provide the program administration with authoritative data on which to make judgments about establishing a program priority around the particular social problem area, and (3) provide data from which to modify program operations to better meet a particular social problem.

PAP was conceived and developed by the Evaluators as a six-step planning process which includes: (1) identification of the problem; (2) analysis of the problem; (3) presenting the data to the Program Administrator in such a way as to allow him to make informed judgments about program planning; (4) designing a plan of action; (5) implementing the plan; and (6) evaluating the results.

The PAP was always prepared in conjunction with the Planning Staff and submitted to the Program Administrator. The Program Administrator responded to the PAP in the form of a written memo, which stated specifically whether the PAP was approved or rejected. If the PAP were rejected, the memo would instruct the staff member as to its final disposition. If approved, the memo would instruct the staff member to design a plan of action, with any additional instructions deemed necessary. The final plan of action then included procedures for implementation and a method of evaluating action impact.

Conclusion

In this chapter we have tried to present an evaluation strategy which represents a point of view and at the same time offers a set of procedures for meeting new standards of accountability in human services delivery.

Traditional evaluation strategies of human services programs have emphasized the measurement of input and process variables, with a view toward determining whether such programs could be launched and sustained in the sense of administrative or political feasibility.

But if the general goal of human services programs is to move people from one level of dependency to a higher level of independence and well-being, then what is needed is a conceptual model of evaluation which emphasizes as the dependent variable the outcome behavior of members of the target group. This requires new "rules of evidence." It is our position that such evidence must derive from indices of improved life chances and mastery over the environment.

An important construct around which our strategy was developed is that behavior is defined in terms of some function of an environmental stimulus. Since change in the behavior of the human services consumer is the goal, then the most effective way of changing his behavior is by changing the environmental circumstances which influence his behavior. Expressed in behavioral terms, one speaks of arranging the environment so that one gets the behavior one wants. These acts of environmental manipulation, then, become the independent variables that we study. Stated as an hypothesis: The essential goal of a social service act or intervention is to change the conditions to which people are responding. If this is done, then people will behave differently.

It is our position that one of the rules of evidence is that goals of human services programs must have their origins in the needs of those to be served and that such needs must be documented in terms of *universe of needs.* In a quantitative sense, the universe of need becomes the constitutive denominator. Evaluation measures, then, test the reduction of needs over time; this in turn is interpreted as an index of improved life chances or mastery over the environment.

Perhaps the most basic attribute of the strategy with respect to accountability of service delivery is the underlying assumption that those who are receiving services should influence the goals and purposes of those delivering services— both at the point of goal determination and at the point of evaluating the services delivered.

Footnotes for Chapter 6

[1] National Commission on Technology, Automation and Economic Progress, Technology and the American Economy (Washington, D. C.: U. S. Government Printing Office, 1966).

[2] S. Gardner, et al. *Services Integration in HEW: An Initial Report,* HEW, U. S. Government Report, 1971.

[3] *Ibid.*

[4] J. B. Turner, "Forgotten: Mezzo-System Intervention." In E. Mullen, Jr., J.

R. Dumpson, & Associates (eds.), *Evaluation of Social Intervention.* (Washington: Jossey-Bass, 1972).

[5] D. G. Gil, "A Systematic Approach to Social Policy Analysis." *The Social Service Review*, Vol. 44, No. 4 (December 1970).

[6] G. Welty, "The Logic of Evaluation." Monograph, (Educational Resources Institute, Chatham College, 1969).

[7] E. Suchman, *Evaluative Research.* (New York: Russel Sage Foundation, 1967).

[8] *Ibid.*

[9] W. Bateman, "Assessing Program Effectiveness." *Welfare in Review*, Vol. 6, No. 1 (January 1968).

[10] Herbert H. Hyman, Charles R. Wright and Terence Hopkins, "Applications of Methods of Evaluation: Four Studies of the Encampment of Citizenship," *University of California Publications in Culture and Society* (Berkeley: University of California Press, 1962).

[11] L. Goodwin, "On Making Social Research Relevant to Social Policy and National Problem Solving," *American Psychologist*, Vol. 26, no. 5 (May 1971).

[12] M. Kaplan, et. al., *Integration of Human Services in HEW.* Vol. I, Report to HEW, (SRS) 73-02012, 1972.

CHAPTER 7

Retardation, Normalization and Evaluation

Joseph J. Parnicky

Services for individuals who are classified as mentally retarded, not unlike those for persons with other disabilities, have in the past shown little concern with evaluation. In retrospect it would appear that, "operating an agency was often equated with rendering a service; and both were equated with rendering quality services."[1] The basic conviction that human services are somehow distinct from other modes of endeavors, such as commercial and industrial, along with the lack of strategies to measure the quality and benefit of human services undoubtedly were prominent factors in deterring efforts at evaluation.

For one, the field of mental retardation is a junior member among the services provided handicapped human beings. "The first significant indication in modern times of informed concern for the mentally retarded—or idiots, as they were generically designated—occurred toward the middle of the nineteenth century."[2] The prognosis for individuals designated as retarded has characteristically been one of hopelessness and irreversibility. The pessimistic perceptions undoubtedly have lessened the pressures for producing positive results and improvements in service systems for the retarded.

Moreover, the field has been heavily weighted by standardized instruments and fixated on measuring the intellectual performance of individuals starting with the pioneer efforts of Binet and others in the early 1900's.[3] When an individual's quotients did not change between testings, it was contended that the results were proof of the impermeability of retardation. When scores did increase, some credit was ascribed to the services provided with at best tentative rationales offered in support of such conclusions.

Another aspect that has contributed to the slow development of service evaluation is the incapability of the client population to voice their own needs, concerns and hopes. It is only in recent decades that their chief advocates—their parents—have organized themselves and become an influential force for examining the nature of services rendered their offspring and for taking concerted action to produce changes.

One strategy for effecting changes in programs and for calling program personnel to task for deficiencies has been through class action suits instituted by parents and other advocates. An increasing number of judicial decisions have affirmed retarded persons' right to treatment. While the courts have not deemed it their role to defining what constitutes appropriate treatment, it is evident that they are not declining to rule on what is inadequate treatment.

Agencies serving the retarded are increasingly being affected by new requirements of funding sources, particularly at the federal and state levels, demanding not only fiscal accountability but programmatic accountability. Audits are no longer limited to an examination of the business office ledgers; they are being expanded to include reviews of educational, social, medical and other services incorporated in the funded programs.

Responses to the "increasing sentiment that human services should account in a better way for the stewardship"[4] in the field of mental retardation are evident along several directions. Accreditation of residential services is a responsibility that has been recently put into effect by the Accreditation Council for Facilities for the Mentally Retarded of the Joint Commission on Accreditation of Hospitals.[1]

Another responsive thrust is in adapting evaluation models from the field of industrial management—i.e., cost-benefit, PPBS (Planning, Programming and Budgeting System) etc.—to the field of mental retardation. One such effort conducted at Kansas University under federal sponsorship has developed a technical assistance network for planning services and building evaluation criteria into services for the developmentally disabled. The techniques developed by Budde[6] and his associates are based upon the following acountability model:

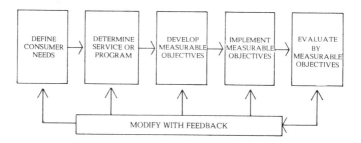

The package includes a needs assessment system, entitled *The Status of Developmental Disabilities Services* (SDDS), which is used to: "(1) determine service needs of known consumer population by geographic area; and (2) locate previously unidentified consumer population by geographic area and specify their service needs. A complimentary manual, *Systematic Planning with Evaluation Criteria* (SPEC), details procedures to: "(1) match services to needs; (2) set priorities for service selection; (3) select services by priority and allocation of assets; (4) coordinate service flow and specify responsibility; (5) specify measurable service criteria; (6) specify timetables for achieving objectives."[7]

In contrast to the above approaches to accountability and evaluation, another has emerged that is more uniquely related to the field of retardation and therefore will be the primary focus of this presentation. This technique for human service accounting rests fundamentally on a conception of retardation as deviancy and a central objective of normalization. Diagramatically this assessment model can be conceived as follows:

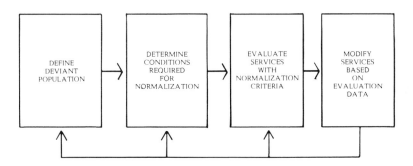

In the 1973 edition of the "Manual on Terminology and Classification in Mental Retardation" the following definition is proposed: "Mental Retardation refers to significantly subaverage general intellectual functioning existing concurrently with deficits in adaptive behavior and manifested during the developmental period."[8] Within the decade since the previous edition[9] the definition was modified to delete the borderline category. Statistically this means that the incidence within the general population was reduced from approximately 15% to 3%!This is but a sample of how widely the term has been defined and applied. Increasingly it is conceded that, "Mental retardation is a diverse condition which stems from an assortment of etiological sources, covers a wide range of functional impairment, and is attended by extremely varied social problems and issues."[10]

Among the newer perspectives applied to mental retardation is one derived from sociology: *deviance*. "With the development of labelling theory, the recognition has come that deviance is a property that is conferred upon an individual by other people."[11] If mental retardation is in the eyes of the beholder to any extent, then it follows that to that extent at least attention should be given to behaviors and characteristics which cause an individual to be marked as a deviant by those observing him.

Wolfensberger with conviction proposes that the strategy for enabling retarded persons to dispel the appearance of deviancy is: *normalization*.[12] The origin of this approach is credited to Bank-Mikkelsen who perceived this as "letting the mentally retarded obtain an existence as close to the normal as possible."[13] Nirje elaborated the idea by stating that normalization is "making available to the mentally retarded patterns and conditions of everyday life which are as close as possible to the norms and patterns of the mainstream of society."[14]

Adapting the Scandinavian orientation, Wolfensberger proposes that the definition of the term is: "Utilization of means which are culturally normative as possible, or order to establish and/or maintain personal behaviors and characteristics which are as culturally normative as possible."[15] He further expands that, "the term 'normative' is intended to have statistical rather than moral connotations, and could be equated with 'typical' or 'conventional.' The phrase 'as culturally normative as possible' implies ultimately an empirical process of determining what and how much is possible."[16] Schematically, Wolfensberger indicates that the principle can be conceived as having two dimensions and three levels of action (Figure 1).

Figure 1
A Schema of the Expression of the Normalization Principle*

Levels of action   Dimensions of Action

	Interaction	Interpretation
Person	Eliciting, shaping, and maintaining normative skills and habits in persons by means of direct physical and social interaction with them	Presenting, managing, addressing, labelling, and interpreting individual persons in a manner emphasizing their similarities to rather than differences from others
Primary and intermediate social systems	Eliciting, shaping, and maintaining normative skills and habits in persons by working indirectly through their primary and intermediate social systems, such as family, classroom, school, work setting, service agency, and neighborhood	Shaping, presenting, and interpreting intermediate social systems surrounding a person or consisting of target persons so that these systems as well as the persons in them are perceived as culturally normative as possible
Societal systems	Eliciting, shaping, and maintaining normative behavior in persons by appropriate shaping of large societal social systems, and structures such as entire svhool systems, laws, and government.	Shaping cultural values attitudes, and stereotypes so as to elicit maximal feasible cultural acceptance of differences.

*Wolfensberg, *op. cit.* 1972, p. 32.

The interaction dimension refers to the retarded individual directly; while the interpretation dimension refers to the way such individual is perceived by others. The person level refers to one-to-one relations, individual retarded persons with individual managers, i.e., teacher, therapist, boss. The primary and intermediate social system level includes the retarded person's family, peer group, neighborhood, fellow workers. The final level, societal systems, is concerned with educational systems, legal systems, welfare systems, mores of the society and the like.

Wolfensberger notes that "we appear to be much more effective in shaping skills to be physically adaptive than in shaping them to be socially normative." [17] At the person level, to escape being considered deviant, it is not enough for a child to be taught to dress, he must be helped to acquire dress habits that are typical in the community. Moreover, managers may need to take an active role in helping the retarded individual present himself normally—as in assisting him in his choice of clothing should he be incapable of doing so himself.

Within the second level, the normalization principle highlights the importance that the group experiences of the retarded encourage non-deviant behaviors and provide maximal exposure to non-deviant individuals. This means living in a bisexual world and carrying out daily routines that approximate those commonly undertaken by others in his age range.

With reference to the third level, Wolfensberger remarks: "Perhaps the major challenge in the interpretational dimension of the societal level is to achieve redefinition of deviance, and to foster greater acceptance of some behaviors or characteristics considered deviant today." [18] He repeatedly stresses that maximal integration of the retarded or deviant person into the social mainstream is a major corollary of the principle of normalization. "Ultimately integration is only meaningful if it is social integration; i.e., if it involves social interaction and acceptance, and not merely physical presence. However, social integration can only be attained if certain preconditions exist, among these being physical integration, although physical integration by itself will not guarantee social integration." [19]

Converting normalization concepts into a procedure for assessing agency performance is obviously a major task. It is just such a conversion that Wolfensberger and Glenn undertake in designing PASS, an acronym for *Program Analysis of*

Service Systems. In addition to providing a schema for measuring quality of services across agency lines and changes over time, the authors propose that it be used as a tool for allocating funds and for teaching the principles of normalization.

Figure 2
Normalization Assessment of Services*

PASS

Category	Score
I. Ideology (34 Items)	840
Physical integration	
Social integration	
Age-appropriate interpretations	
and structures	
Culture-appropriate interpretations	
and structures	
Specialization	
Developmental growth orientation	
Quality of setting	
II. Administration (7 items)	160
Manpower considerations	
Operational effectiveness	
Total:	1,000

FUNDET

Category	Score
I. Continuation of funding (5 items)	700
Hardship factors	
Financial need	
Socio-ecological hardship	
Geo-demographic hardship	
II. Funder priorities (3 items)	300
Client appropriateness	
Program appropriateness	
Consistency with funder	
policies and standards	
Total:	1,000

*Per Wolfensberger, *op. cit.,* 1973, pp. 224-226.

PASS (Figure 2) identifies 4l items pertaining to aspects of program quality to be rated. Each item is scored on four to six levels, with the lowest signifying unacceptable quality and the highest approaching ideal conditions. The manual provides detailed statements on which ratings are to be assigned. The scoring weights were designated on an *a priori* basis, with 840 points maximum for items related to normalization aspects and 160 points maximum for administrative matters. The total score of 1000 points can also be computed into a program score and a physical facility score.

Complimenting PASS is a schedule for scoring aspects of the agency which have a bearing on funding but do not directly relate to quality of service. This subsystem, called FUNDET (for Funding Determination) contains eight items, but is also scored on a maximum of 1000 points. This score is proposed as a basis for differential decisions regarding funding service programs with relatively equal PASS scores.

PASS-FUNDET evaluations can be administered by agency personnel, but the recommended technique is for such evaluation to be undertaken by no less than three raters, who are free of involvement in the program being rated. In addition to written manuals, check lists and the text on normalization, a series of workshops are being conducted by Wolfensberger and Glenn to train raters in the principles and the procedures. Professional background is not considered essential, but "raters must have high intelligence and communication skills."[21] Ratings are based on written materials submitted by program personnel and on a site visit. Raters are instructed to conduct site visits and interviews jointly so they are rating common elements of the service program. However, their ratings are to be made independently. After the evaluations are completed, the scores on each of the items are averaged in determining the overall quality of the program.

As an example of the rating guides, the following are the distinctions for the six scores of the item concerned with: "socially integrative social opportunities":

LEVEL 1 projects are those in which the clients have very little opportunity to interact and engage in culturally normative activities and contexts appropriate for the individuals being served. In most instances, this implies a virtually total lack of culturally typical activities in culturally typical settings, in close contact with ordinary citizens in any of the four areas.

LEVEL 2 projects include some socially integrative opportunities . . . but their quantity and quality are either too selective or inappropriately limited. To be rated on this level, projects must provide at least a moderate amount of culturally-typical engagements in one, and some engagements in another of the four areas.

LEVEL 3 projects provide opportunities for socially integrative engagements to a moderate degree in at least two areas, and some in one other of the four major areas.

LEVEL 4 projects are those where extensive provisions are made for clientele to interact and engage in culturally normative activities and contexts in at least three areas, and at least some in the fourth.

LEVEL 5 projects provide extensive opportunities for socially integrative opportunities in all four areas, but with further improvements being obviously possible.

LEVEL 6 applies to those projects which provide such extensive and imaginative opportunities for social integration in all four areas of functioning that with our current ideology, further improvement can not be readily conceptualized.[22]

The first version of PASS was used in Nebraska in 1970 and 1971 as a basis for determining which community services for mental retarded clients were to be funded.[23] Seven service agencies were evaluated by this technique on both occasions. "Most gratifying support for the validity of PASS was provided by the finding that the number of retarded clients who moved from a less advanced to a more advanced status (e.g., from training to independent employment) correlated at a highly significant .96 with total PASS scores. The correlation between ideology and administration ratings was a high .78."[24] The authors also conclude that the results appear to be supported by subsequent observations of the evaluated Nebraska programs and that the application of PASS "may have been a major force in completely depoliticizing the allocation of funds."[25] The data obtained from the original version served as the bases for expanding and revising the PASS technique. Reports indicate that this evaluation scheme is being adopted by a variety of service agencies in Canada as well as in the United States.

The designers of the technique realize that this evaluation procedure relies heavily on the judgments of the raters. They contend that application of the normalization principle cannot be determined by merely counting showers or measuring rooms. They are convinced that "standardizing" the raters so that they understand the PASS system, its underlying tenets as well as its scoring gradients is not only possible but also the method of choice in evaluating programs.

The development of the normalization approach to evaluation concurrently with procedures stemming from management models suggests that complimentary assessments might be obtained by applying both to a particular program of human services. The normalization method would provide data derived from criteria applicable across agencies; while the management method would furnish measures based on objectives determined for the particular agency program. Comparative utility of information gained from each of these approaches might well contribute to the advancement of accountability in the field of human services. The following illustrates such application of both models to service evaluation:

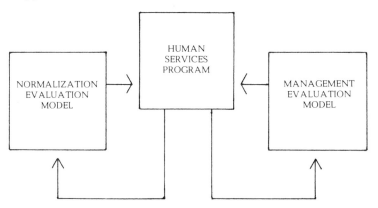

It is even conceivable that feedback from one model could be useful in revisiting the other.

Obviously the normalization-evaluation technique is still in an early stage of development and will need to be tested much more extensively—and by researchers who have not had a hand in its conception. Nevertheless, it offers a contrasting approach to human service accounting. Rather than drawing from industrial management models, it draws primarily from the social sciences, from conceptions of mental retardation, deviance and normalization. Although designed to yield numerical ratings, it depends heavily on informed judgments rather than statistical information for its measurements of service quality. While considered adaptable to local conditions, the technique strives to define criteria that can be applied comparatively across agencies, programs and services. Within parameters set forth by the normalization assessment technique, there are unquestionably problems of validity and objectivity; but given its underlying purpose—the universal application of the principle of normalization for the welfare of retarded persons—one can only hope that further experimentation and refinement will make the goal achievable.

Footnotes for Chapter 7

[1] W. Wolfensberger & L. Glenn, *Program Analysis of Service Systems: Handbook.* (Toronto, Canada: National Institute of Mental Retardation, 1973) p. 2.

[2] M. Adams, *Mental Retardation and Its Social Dimensions.* (New York: Child Welfare League of America, 1971), p. 17.

[3] G. D. Stoddard, *The Meaning of Intelligence,* (New York: Macmillan, 1947).

[4] W. Wolfensberger & L. Glenn, *Op. Cit.,* 1973, p. 2.

[5] Accreditation Council for Facilities for the Mentally Retarded *Standards for Residential Facilities for the Mentally Retarded* (Chicago: Joint Commission on Accreditation of Hospitals, 1971).

[6] J. F. Budde, E. Eklund & J. Hanna *Formative Management* Mimeographed Lawrence, Kan.: Univeristy of Kansas, 1973), p. 6.

[7] J. F. Budde, J. Hanna & E. Eklund. *Systematic Planning with Evaluation Criteria.* (condensed). (Lawrence, Kan.: University of Kansas, 1973), pp. 4-5.

[8] H. J. Grossman ed. *Manual on Terminology and Classification in Mental Retardation* (Washington, D. C.: American Association on Mental Deficiency, 1973) p.11.

[9] R. Heber. ed. *Manual on Terminology and Classification in Mental Retardation,* (Washington, D. C.: American Association on Mental Deficiency, 1961).

[10] Adams, *Op. Cit.,* p. 1.

[11] R. A. Scott & J. D. Douglas, *Theoretical Perspectives on Deviance* (New York: Basic Books, 1972) p. 11.

[12] W. Wolfensberger, *The Principle of Normalization in Human Services* (Toronto, Canada: National Institute on Mental Retardation, 1972).

[13] N. E. Bank-Mikkelsen, "A Metropolitan area in Denmark: Copenhagen, *"Changing Patterns in Residential Service for the Mentally Retarded,* ed. R. Kugel & W. Wolfensberger (Washington, D. C.: President's Committee on Mentally Retarded, 1969) p. 234.

[14] B. Nirge, "The Normalization principle and its human management implications," In R. Kugel & W. Wolfensberger, 1969, p. 181.

[15] Wolfensberger, 1972 *Op. Cit.* p. 28.

[16] *Ibid.*

[17] *Wolfensberger, 1972, p. 33.*

[18] *Wolfensberger, 1972, p. 40.*

[19] *Wolfensberger, 1972, p. 48.*

[20] *Wolfensberger and Glenn, 1973.*

164 Evaluation and Accountability

[21] *Wolfensberger and Glenn, 1973, p. 12.*

[22] W. *Wolfensberger and L. Glenn, Programm Analysis of Service Systems: Field Manual* (Toronto, Canada: National Institute on Mental Retardation, 1973) p. 19.

[23] B. Macy, *Analysis of 1970 and 1971 PASS Scores* (Lincoln, Nebraska: Nebraska Office of Mental Retardation, 1971.)

[24] Wolfensberger & Glenn, 1973, p.7.

[25] *Ibid.*

CHAPTER 8

Strains on Objectivity in Community
Focused Research With Runaways

Rocco D'Angelo

Very often attempts on the part of a researcher to propose evaluation of social programs generate fears of imminent extinction. These sensations frequently arise out of the confrontation between a funding group and a well-meaning applicant for research funds. A vision is conjured up in the mind of the researcher which depicts a courtroom scene in which the researcher is assigned—with great misgivings—the role of a defendent. He is temporarily relieved to know that he is represented in the proceedings by a highly experienced Charity League lawyer of unimpeachable character and distinguished credentials. In the dream, the funding source assumes the guise of the plaintiff. Some discomfort is experienced when it is learned that the plaintiff is represented by a dashing, young, inexperienced but opportunistic lawyer of Sterling Law School vintage. The look of determination and suave confidence displayed by the young lawyer terrifies the defendent. He knows that the outcome of the trial, for all intents and purposes, will be determined by the callousness or shrewdness of the lawyers. If not by the lawyers, the outcome could be determined by the rules of trial established by the court judge (a political appointee of whom he is suspicious) and which may be completely irrelevant to the crucial issues. The point of this exaggerated illustration is that the research funding process can evoke deep reactions of defensiveness on the part of the researcher. Doubting himself, he may be induced to search for flaws in what he is planning to do in order to placate groups which provide financial backing for research proposals. Knowing this reaction, potential sponsors of research sometimes engage in the practice of nit-picking for the purpose of influencing the designs of research projects. The defensive stance of a researcher may play into the sponsor group's attempt to manipulate the research process and thereby raise the issue of methodological contamination. The purpose of this article is to examine specific illustrations of manipulation in social research and to note the effects on methodological objectivity. Illustrations are drawn from the Teenage Flight Project[1].

In the Fall of 1972, the Teenage Flight Project was initiated in Columbus, Ohio. The project was conceived as a comprehensive two-year research and community action effort designed to accomplish two research objectives. The first objective was to develop a behavior profile of teenage runaways in the Central Ohio area; the second was to assess the effectiveness of community facilities for handling runaways and their problems. The role of descriptive studies in assessing goals and existing conditions is invaluable to social policy development.[2] In this instance the overall goal of the project was to improve community programs which deal with teenage runaways. The project received broad community support from its inception and was successful in gaining small-scale funding sufficient to carry out the project goals from three local foundations. In addition to financial support, the project incorporated community participation in three ways:

1. Local institutions cooperated by supplying adolescent subjects (a runaway group and a control group of non-runaways) for interviews and by supplying data that would make it possible to assess service effectiveness.

2. College trained volunteers served as research workers for the profile study and administered the agency effectiveness survey.

3. Representatives from interested community groups served on an advisory board and various task forces that analyzed the research data and evaluated findings.

The project was committed to the concept of community participation in research methodology as well as social action strategy. This approach to social problem solving was termed *community action research* and it employed the use of consensus groups in progressive stages. Freeman and Sherwood have reported that legislative and regulatory bodies are increasingly demanding that "expert" views be collated before framing public programs. [3] The concept of expertness, however, poses issues on which consensus is rarely achieved. Since the popularization of the consumer advocacy movement in the early 1960's, the notion of elitism in social programing has aroused public suspicion and fears of professional opportunism. To avoid such pitfalls in this study, it was recognized that expertness can be legitimized from several vantage points. The concept was defined so as to include the participations of youths, parents, teachers, ministers, professional counselors and others with plausible views on the problem of runaways.

Having opened up the project to broad participation, it became necessary to differentiate the roles of professional research staff and those of volunteer workers or community participants. Research personnel were assigned responsibilities having to do with methodological concerns including study design, sampling and instrumentation, training and supervision of volunteer personnel, organization and statistical evaluation of data and report writing. Volunteer personnel carried responsibilities in numerous areas including data collection, data tabulation, non-statistical analysis, analysis of findings and explication of recommendations. In the follow-up phase of the project, volunteers carried a number of community actions as "catalytic agents." They became active in community education, community organization, consumer advocacy, negotiations with agencies and—generally speaking—in the process of implementation of change. Some of the obstacles encountered in this project were related to the community-oriented feature of the undertaking. Because community participation was so pervasive in this research, the opportunity for interferences cropping up in the process was everpresent. Some of the obstacles encountered in the research process are discussed in the sections which follow.[4]

People Pressures
On Research

The concept of community participation created a number of predictable confrontations that produced sour notes early in the research process. One expects community reactions to a social research project. However, complications due to the variety of motives that induce individuals and groups to cooperate or not to cooperate are not easily foreseeable. One regular source of interferences in the Teenage Flight Project was instigated by political considerations — an area frequently underestimated by innocent researchers out of a genuine desire to remain objective. One example of the numerous instances in this category involved a school administrator who was approached and asked to cooperate in the selection of a control sample needed to conduct the study. After being given a copy of the study questionnaire (which he requested) and reacting to items having to do with parent-child interaction, the administrator expressed his reluctance to cooperate out of fear that "political pressure" would be brought upon him by irate parents. [5] When the unlikelihood of such an outcome was explained—because it was required that parental consent in written form be obtained as a condition of student participation—instead of expressing relief, the school official's temper escalated into a protest over the fact that his school had been selected for the controversial study. Needless to say, this reaction convinced the researchers of the advisability of looking elsewhere for more fertile ground. An immediate problem arose related to sample composition because of the stratification procedures used to insure representation of different racial types in the study. Fortunately, a suitable replacement school was found that satisfied all the essential criteria. This minor incident resensitized the senior researcher to the political maneuverings that persisted—directly and by proxy—in the seemingly endless competition with the research process.

There is another interesting form of pressure operating on researchers caused by people or groups desiring to guide the research outcomes by setting up some kind of monitoring system. This may take the form of a blatant attempt to dictate findings through some external agency imposing its views on the research data. One approach taken by an anxious sponsor of the Teenage Flight Project was to insist that an editorial board be appointed to oversee the preparation of the research report. While the active involvement of the sponsor in the research process is ordinarily viewed as unacceptable, the community action focus of the teenage project became a rationale for departing from conventional practice. A compromise was negotiated in the way of assigning a board of community agency representatives an advisory role in reviewing and commenting on (minority report fashion) the research findings. What seemed on the surface a major methodological concession, in retrospect, offered a new opportunity to expand the data base. The responses of informed community agents offered gains in validity. [6] Their reactions were also construed as "new data" (community reactions to results) on a secondary level that provided depth valued although not anticipated in the original design. The idea seemed so appealing that a second monitoring panel consisting of a representative group of teenagers who participated as subjects in the research was established. The understanding that groups responses were to be incorporated into the research report produced a favorable boost in the morale of some resistant community groups.

Nevertheless, researchers should remain wary of power groups whose motives may not always be altruistic in the end. Departing for a moment to the broader scene, it would be instructive to compare these outcomes to another monitoring situation reported in Daniel P. Moynihan's recently published book describing the political background that surrounded President Nixon's unsuccessful Family Assistance Plan (FAP).[7] The federal government sponsored the New Jersey Graduate Work Incentive Experiment, conducted by the University of Wisconsin's Institute for Research on Poverty in conjunction with Mathematica, Inc. A four-year experiment was planned from 1968 to 1972, testing out a variety of approaches to income maintenance on a "scientific" plan.

> ...it was to be completed in 1972. Events in a sense, overran it. Well before it was completed, a president had embraced its principles and its hoped-for conclusions, to the extent at least of deciding that "graduated work incentive" system could hardly be worse than "welfare." Inevitably there arose a conflict between methodological demands of social science and the political needs of Congress and the Administration, and, perhaps, just as inevitably the latter won out.[8]

Under pressure from mounting resistance to their favored income maintenance proposal, the Nixon Administration arranged to "break into" the data from the New Jersey study late in 1969 in order to obtain "preliminary" information that would have a favorable and supportive effect on FAP. Moynihan reported that 509 of 1,359 participating families in the study were "examined" and the results reported to a Cabinet meeting on February 18, 1970.[9] The question of interference with the research process was so blatant in that instance as to leave suspect whatever findings were reported. To what degree did the researchers feel free to depart from the "preliminary" results favored by the President in their conclusions?

There is another form of intrusion in the research process which takes the shape of a gift horse. This is a situation where it is insisted by the sponsor group that certain amenities be provided as a condition to sanctioning the research. The predicament is compounded when the research project happens to be community oriented since every participant legitimately views himself as a sponsor. The illustrations varied and some seem comical in the recounting. One cooperative agency insisted on accommodating the research team with a special room so as to avoid any clashes with regular in-house activity. Unfortunately, the researchers frequently found the room locked and the key was not always readily available. For lack of space in one large institution, a research interviewer was forced to conduct an interview with a teenage subject in the janitor's closet. A public agency official (elected) boasted that he was a great supporter of research and promised to give his full cooperation to facilitate the research on the condition that nothing negative was printed about his institution. The most notable situation, however, concerns the demand by one of the funding groups made in the form of an offer. The request seemed harmless at first—simply that some of its college educated members be used and trained in the research process. There was no question about the competence level of the volunteers. Nevertheless, what seemed to evolve resembled a reversal of the "Peter's Bridge" concept referred to in *The Peter Principle*.[10] As the cooperation effort progressed, the organization seemed to develop the complex machinery of a full-scale military operation. The research process had to be modified in order to accommodate the need for constant retraining and management of volunteer personnel. Questionnaires had to be simplified and closely checked to maintain uniformity, resulting in some loss of valued data. Research staff were delegated supervisory roles and became mediators in interpersonal disputes between volunteers which often distracted them from their business. While the arrangement worked out in the end, it seemed that instead of giving something to the research, the volunteers took something away from it. The research process became secondary to control of people.

Community Attitudes
And The Research Enterprise

The primary vulnerability of community action research may in fact be that which is its most apparent asset—the community interaction process. Previous illustrations have demonstrated the effects of community attitudes on the course of the Teenage Flight Project. A key question arising from this discussion is: Were these incidents entirely the product of the particular methodology employed in the research project? There is reason to think not. In order to more fully respond to the question, it would be profitable to switch to a broader perspective and to take notice of how community attitudes interact with the general research enterprise.

During the past two decades, the field of research has been changed by an increasing reliance on machine processing of information. Computer technology has revolutionized all fields of learning. Not only has the computer advanced the timetable of scientific progress, but it has been responsible for the creation of new disciplines of academic learning which emerged from the proliferation of information. One of the attitudinal effects of the data revolution has been the notion that there exists a more-than-usable supply of information or "data gluts." While the need for social science information may be at an unprecedented peak, the community is able and willing to invest in only so much research. Just as we have accumulated stockpiles of grains and weapons in recent years, members of the community have acquired the notion that researchers are stockpiling information into a useless reserve. Such attitudes shape the demands that funding groups make on researchers. Awed by the vision of spinning reels of computer data tapes, some groups have lost their sense of urgency about sponsoring social research. Having minimized the need for such, these funding bodies have exercised the option of pursuing their idiosyncratic interests instead of the public good. This situation has placed restrictions on the field of competition for social researchers since the bulk of funded projects stem from a relatively select group of private and public sources. Consequently, success-hungry grant writers have had to become more concerned about the tastes and needs of contractors and less concerned about knowledge gaps. The upshot has been some wastage of valuable technical resources on the pursuit of superficial issues, according to Andreski.

Even when no vested interests are affected, factual findings may be enthusiastically welcomed or vehemently criticized simply because they pander to, or offend, current preconceptions, even if these are cherished for no other reason than sheer mental inertia. The fashionable craving for novelty makes no basic difference because it only leads to a chase after superficial innovations which demand no mental effort. As we shall see later, this is the reason why purely verbal innovations easily gain popularity.[11]

Research Costs On
The Practitioner's Side

There are other cost effects that stem from public attitudes that regard new research efforts as surplus commodities. Consider the cost impact on the researcher who must necessarily relate to the data entrepreneurs! The research practitioner's reaction is understandably conservative, i.e., bent on conserving his own energy. An example of this reaction is provided by what Andreski labels "hiding behind methodology."[12] This technique is practiced by those who insist on methodological perfection of such an order that it precludes giving attention to any but the most trivial issues. Funding committees can be surprisingly responsive to methodological approaches. Their reactions provide profits and ego trips for shrewd practitioners focused on material gain. While methodological approaches result in great quantities of data with very little mental initiative, the analysis of data tends to be superficial and inadequate to serve any long range purpose.

While technology has reduced the cost of generating monotonous data, the researcher has had to contend with demands for sophistication and rigorous training as a right of passage. At the same time, concentrations of large firms in the publishing enterprise have reduced, relatively, the number of openings for authors because of their discouragement of unorthodox views. Andreski has noted that research which focuses attention on basic institutions such as courts, religion, the family, and political bodies—because of possible offense to consumer groups—is likely to curry disfavor and criticism for "non-scientific" propositions. The absence of absolute controls in the methodology of sociological researchers plays into public skepticism and provides a rationalization for many groups to remain complacent about social problems. The social science market, concludes Andreski, is enslaved by commercial preference for publications which demand little effort and do not offend widespread prejudice.[13]

The additional burden that researchers in the social sciences have to carry in contrast to physical scientists, with their seemingly unlimited access to experimentation and instrumentation, deserves one last comment. In a recently published reprint of an early publication of essays delivered to the staff and research fellows of the Brookings Institution, this handicap was clearly characterized. William I. Thomas, a well known scholar during the depression period, recorded his perception of the difference between what he termed resistance to change in the physical sciences compared to the social sciences:

> In social science the problem is not mainly the control of the material world but of the behavior of individuals as members of society. The subject matter of the social sciences is in fact behavior, fundamentally. And here experimentation with the human materials is limited, and resistance to change is more stubborn on account of the sanctity of the custom and the rivalry of personal interests. [14]

Some observers have become so disturbed by issues of outside control of research that fears have been raised regarding our loss of political control over the course of our technology. This perception is disputed by Calder who considers American-based science to be constrained by intellectual promiscuity. [15] He found that much innovation which revolutionizes an industry often originates with obscure, low echelon employees. The inventor and technological entrepreneur trigger the innovation process, but there are many steps between them. A new idea needs to be evaluated in many dimensions of cost before it is completely accepted.Decisions have to be made pertaining to research investment, production factors, effects on the competitive market, and so on. A new idea can be a very expensive proposition. Therefore, the market-oriented society demands that cost and profit considerations must prevail in innovation rather than the quality of the researcher's contribution.

Reflections and Conclusions

This article has examined a number of obstacles that pose a threat to the conduct of objective research at different levels of research intervention. Identified obstacles to objective research included the defensiveness of the researcher, demands by outside groups wishing to exert control over the research outcomes, increasing costs to the researcher of doing research and commercialism on the part of entrepreneurial groups. Whatever their source, such challenges deserve our attention since they represent compromising pressures on methodological objectivity. In one particular illustration from the Teenage Flight Project, a concession in the form of permitting monitoring panels to be imposed on the research process, produced gains in innovation and enhanced validity. Reference to a national study drawn from Moynihan's book, *The Politics of a Guaranteed Income*, revealed how the intense interest of a president monitored a guaranteed income experiment, destroying the credibility of the objectiveness of findings. Eventually, we are led to the conclusion that gains as well as losses can be sustained in the rivalry between research sponsor interests and the methodological independence of the researcher. If this is true, perhaps there is some measure of consolation in regarding what Calder termed intellectual promiscuity as a passing phase of phylogenic adaptation. In the realm of the natural sciences, the concept of evolution of form in response to new environmental pressures is recognized as resulting in new strains which can be advantageous to a given species in the long run. Perhaps this interpretation has relevance here.

Researchers are understandably cynical about the market approach to funding because of the depreciation effect it has on methodology—the research practitioner's sacred symbol. The thought of changing idols is a painful prospect to the most faithful. But can researchers afford to disregard the demands of influential consumers without running the risk of professional extinction? Is it possible that social researchers have been too resistant to pressures for change because of trivial biases? Have the social sciences relied too heavily on the methodologies of the physical sciences at the expense of developing new forms? In order to be served by knowledge, society needs to be in a position to distinguish what it knows. It is this need to explicate the real world, rather than the particular form used in conducting a social inquiry, that provides the primary defense for research. The researcher is motivated by his thirst for new knowledge toward the end of creating a body of theoretical constructs which will delineate the general relationships of the empirical world. [16] The challenge posed by uncertainty should motivate social researchers, as well, to confront the methodological issues and to attempt to resolve them honestly. By avoiding confrontations, advances in methodology are deferred. As it stands, pressures from the market place will continue to serve as a sieve to test the relevance and utility of research efforts until a better system can be found.

Footnotes for Chapter 8

[1] The author is director of the Teenage Flight Project and associate professor of social work at The Ohio State University. The project was staffed by a field unit consisting of three second-year graduate social work students and a doctoral student in home economics.

[2] Howard E. Freeman and Clarence C. Sherwood, *Social Research and Social Policy* (New Jersey: Prentice Hall, Inc., 1970), p. 138.

[3] *Ibid.*, pp. 37-38.

[4] A more detailed description of the research project and its findings will become available in the near future. A monograph of the Teenage Flight Project study entitled *Families of Sand* is scheduled to be published by the School of Social Work of The Ohio State University in 1974.

[5] Some items on the questionnaire pertained to mother-father interaction, disciplinary measures, religious practices and attitudes. The school in question was one of a number of schools in the capital city that had experienced integration struggles in the past. The claim of the administrator that he would be under political pressure was speculative and, probably, presumptuous. Subsequent experiences involving other schools in the same system turned out highly successful. In a different community, the school principal required that all parents of children involved in the study be contacted personally by the researchers. Despite initial anxieties, it was accomplished in good order.

[6] The validity of measuring instruments is judged by the extent to which their results are compatible with other relevant evidence. The truthfulness of data and, therefore, their credibility is enhanced by complementarity in the researcher's measurements with the observations of community groups. Such corroborating evidence is testimonial in nature. See discussion in: Selltiz, Clair, et al., *Research Methods In Social Relations* (New York: Holt, Rinehart & Winston, 1965) p. 156.

[7] Daniel P. Moynihan, *The Politics of a Guaranteed Income* (New York: Random House, 1973).

[8] *Ibid.*, p. 191.

[9] *Ibid.*

[10] The concept refers to a method of rising in the status hierarchy through motivating a prospective patron by persuading him that he has something to gain by assisting you, or something to lose by not assisting you. Dr. Lawrence J. Peter and Raymond Hull *The Peter Principle: Why Things Always Go Wrong* (New York: William Morrow & Co., Inc.,) 1969.

[11] Stanislav Andreski, *Social Science as Sorcery* (New York: St. Martin's Press, 1972) p. 37.

[12] *Ibid.*, p. 109.

[13] *Ibid.*, p. 47.

[14] William I. Thomas, "The Relation of Research to the Social Science Process," in *Essays on Research in the Social Sciences*, ed. Leveret Lyon   (Washington, D. C: The Brookings Institution, 1968) p. 176.

[15] Nigel Calder, *Technopolis, Social Control of the Uses of Science* (New York: Simon & Schuster, 1970), p. 90.

[16] Kenneth Boulding, *Beyond Economics* (Ann Arbor, Michigan: University of Michigan, 1968), pp. 84-85.

PART IV

OVER-ALL COMMENTARY
AND BIBLIOGRAPHY

CHAPTER 9

Evaluating Human Service Programs:
A Critical Overview*

Leonard Schneiderman

One might, in a somewhat cynical tone, attribute part of the current interest in evaluation as well to efforts to use and concept of "effectiveness" as a means for legitimizing administrative decisions made by other means. The President's New Federalism makes it clear that the federal government's role as an equalizer of resources and opportunities among citizens of the United States is to be modified. No a priori national committment is to be made to any specific needy or disadvantaged group, to any narrow categories of people within the society, leaving it instead to state and local communities to establish the social priorities to be used in expanding federal revenues for social purposes. The federal budget is, in turn, to be sharply limited as part of the administration's anti-inflation effort with severe limitations placed on spending for human service programs. This will have special consequences for those groups most dependent upon public spending while leaving private consumption essentially unrestrained through taxation. The result can only be an intensification of already existing social and economic inequities in this society. The discontinuation of social programs becomes much more acceptable if the proposal is not for termination, but rather, for the replacement of programs shown to be "ineffective." Administrative action based on other premises, seeks legitimation through the methods of "objective" analysis. Such decisions, of course, are only peripherally related to measures of effectiveness. They concern issues of value and ideology for which evaluation research is largely irrelevant. No findings are likely to tell us whether investments in foreign or domestic, military or civilian, physical or human resources are

---

*Editors' Note: This overview was based on five major symposium papers which were presented by Warren, Coke and Hansan, Higgs, Weiss, and Nagi. You may note that in this article most direct statements from the above mentioned authors have not been specifically footnoted. However, the sources are identified either before or after the statement so that the reader may be able to refer to the original work, if needed.

better. That ideological and political reality is, no doubt, a good place to begin, and to end, any discussion of "the evaluation of human service programs."

For the purpose of reviewing the papers presented at this symposium (a difficult and perhaps impossible task) I would like to pose and attempt an answer to three questions:

1. What are the speaker's perceptions of the system employing evaluation methodology?

2. What is the role they envision in that system for the evaluator?

3. What methods are available for use by an evaluator so employed?

The three questions are based upon a particular way of looking at the subject. "The evaluator" is seen as one role in a larger system of roles. It is no more possible to understand the "play" of the evaluator without knowledge of the larger system than it is to know what a second baseman is doing, and why, without knowing that he is part of a larger game called baseball. Different perceptions of the larger field of action, of the evaluator's role, are certain to lead to differences in preferred methodology.

All of those presenting papers at the symposium see the human service system as shaped by the needs and values of multiple constituencies with complex purposes and action alternatives. Their perceptions of the evaluator as an actor in the human service system, as someone both reacting to and acting upon the system, overlap, but vary in emphasis, and in some cases, in substance.

While expressed in somewhat different terms, all see the human service system as involving service strategies which are themselves designed to achieve multiple program objectives, some of which are clearly stated and some of which are latent or implied. The goals themselves often conflict and are products of differing ideologies, attaching different valuations to "conflicting constructions of social reality" (Warren). Problem definition, the articulation of goals and objectives, program design strategies and service delivery tactics are all seen as interacting and interrelated, interdependent levels, or parts, of this total system.

Warren expresses this in his principle thesis that conventional evaluation research tends to fragment the problems which the intervention is supposed to address in such a way that the problems become largely insoluble at that level and hence the findings, whether positive or negative, are often largely irrelevant to the problems addressed. By accepting a fragmented agency program as the point of departure for study, the evaluation research also naively accepts the agency's implicit definition of the problem and the nature of the proposed remedies for it. He thus jumps into the evaluation process without having given systematic attention to a critical investigation of the nature of the problem definition and its prescriptive implications for the articulation of program goals and interventive strategies. Warren's concern is illustrated by reference to the tendency of human service programs to define problems as due to the personal deficiencies of persons having those problems, and, as a consequence, to the concomitant preference for treatment and rehabilitative strategies of personal service. Higgs seems impatient with this concern for alternative explanatory systems and for their possible unintended consequences. "If the desired results are there, he is satisfied" (Higgs). The relationship of alternative explanatory systems to a determination of whether or not the results are there is unrecognized. By analogy to the physical world, Higgs presumes that outmoded means, based upon archaic explanatory systems, can have no more detrimental impact upon people than the use of pre-Einsteinian physics on the building of a bridge. It is not the means, but the ends, that count. Does it work?

Weiss sees a human service system involving a set of interconnected and interdependent decision points, namely, policy decisions, strategy decisions and tactical decisions. Once basic policy objectives are set, decisions need to be made on the strategies of intervention to be used, and, on how tactically they can best be translated into services delivered. Each decision point involves different actors, operating at different levels in the system and requires a different order of information to support decision making. The objectives reflect the values and priorities of the program sponsors and therefore, those values need to be understood by the evaluator in order to know the basis on which the sponsor will judge the merit of the program. Objectives may be reflected in the "official goals" of the program or they may be goals involving the political and symbolic functions that programs serve.

At any rate, those who make policy, management and tactical decisions are part of a total system in which particular ideologies and problem conceptualizations generate explicit or implicit objectives which, once set, require a continuing set of interrelated decisions on policy goals, program strategies and service tactics. Nagi's paper is especially useful in its discussion of factors shaping those tactical decisions. Using the market place concepts of supply and demand, he hypothesizes, (1) that when the balance of services, supply and demand is in favor of supply, the organizational tendency will be to accept doubtful applicants; (2) when the balance of services, supply and demand is in favor of demand, the tendency will be to reject doubtful applicants. Some organizations, he observes, react like traditional economic enterprises and increase the charge assessed against clients for service. In social service systems, these charges may involve non-pecuniary costs, as in waiting time spent in clinics or on waiting lists or in the form of restrictive means tests administered to applicants for service.

When supply and demand are out of balance, balance may also be reestablished through the specialization of agency service programs, that is, the segregation of clients into sectors to whom different levels of service are applied; the development of "dumping grounds" in public schools and in the "back wards" of mental hospitals, and in institutions for the mentally retarded are manifestations of this process and of the effort to limit demand to available resources. Nagi cautions us about the lesson to be learned here in connection with the development of a new cadre of para-professionals and a possible emergence of two levels of care, not differentiated by type or complexity of problem but by the social characteristics of applicants.

When service results are relatively quantifiable, a premium according to Nagi, may be placed upon the achievement of those measurable objectives. Management by objective can lead to the selection of clients by objective. This criterion becomes incorporated into the organization's reward system and fosters an avoidance of risks in applicants accepted for services. The quantifiability of results may also lead to goal displacement when success in achieving the emergent goals is more easily measurable than the organization's original goals.

Within the service system as conceptualized above, Weiss' evaluator acts on the principle that no one model of evaluation is suitable for all actors or for all uses. The production of data according to Weiss must be geared to the needs and interests of the user. Only when we design evaluation to fit the needs of decision makers, the issues they face, the information that will clarify the issues, and the salience to them of different kinds of information, do we extend the chance of reaching the goals of evaluation, namely, better human services and wiser allocation of resources among and within programs.

If a program is going to be continued no matter what its failings, it is fruitless to find out that it is ineffective on overall measures of success, but it can be productive to show what kinds of strategy modification would improve its service. Likewise, if certain program strategies are invulnerable to change there can be value in finding out whether there are better means to put strategies into practice (Weiss).

Higgs has a view of a prototypical multi-stage, decision process which, like incrementalism, involves a continuing process of charting and recharting one's course, but, unlike incrementalism, the desired end-state is known and maintained throughout to guide the process of charting and the process of steering and adapting and adjusting to changing conditions. In this process, the actor first takes his present position as given. Next, he articulates a goal and a desired end-state. This end-state must, presumably, be different from what exists. Presumably, also, there are many possible end-states which the actor could imagine. Presumably, also, the one he chooses is a function of what he most values and of what he sees as possible at the moment, and, presumably also, despite the assumption of "changing conditions" his information about new possibilities remains unchanged. His value preferences remain unchanged. His opportunities and resources remain unchanged. What is constant is the desired end–state he seeks and the constancy of values, opportunities and resources that that implies. Thirdly, the actor employs successive approximations each designed to bring him closer to his objective when each successive approximation improves performance, and, finally, throughout the process he obeys the injunction, "do the best you can from where you are" (Higgs). In this process, the researcher/evaluator as actor utilizes the same decision process just articulated.

Higgs' evaluator is an illusive mix of social analyst, research technician, advocacy planner. He uses a wide variety of methods including experimental design and a "prototyping strategy." I must admit to having insufficient time to adequately understand what this means.

Nagi's view seems to be that of an organizational system which involves the interest articulation, interest aggregation, rule making, etc., functions developed in Gabriel Almond's framework—a system in which the research/evaluator operates outside the system as an objective commentator on the products of the system, feeding his findings back to system actors.

While perceptions of the human service system seem similarly based on a rational model, there are major points of difference about the role model for the evaluator within that system. Weiss issues a call to technical competency and to practicality. Higgs does this as well but wants these along with faith in experimental technology and guts in overcoming all technical, political, administrative, moral and ethical problems in its implementation. Warren's is a call for a social diagnostician, for analytical investigation of the total social context surrounding the problem behavior. The method proposed is "informed rational analysis" defined as "trying to put together what we know from social theory, from practice experience and from evaluation efforts in order to assess the general social configuration within which social problems develop" (Warren). This model is not unlike Higgs' extensively described but confusing "prototyping strategy" at least in the first stage of implementation. Warren's strategy is rather ambiguously drawn and certainly difficult to replicate methodologically.

Given the inter-relationship between problem definition, the articulation of program objectives, strategies and service tactics, it is difficult not to share Warren's conclusion that evaluation research in any one part of this system must necessarily impact on all other parts of the system. It does appear critical for the evaluator to accept the reality of his position within, and not outside, the service system being evaluated, and, to accept the further reality that his actions may have both intended and unintended consequences for the total system, including, even, the legitimation of programs on which negative results have been reported. Weiss's view on evaluative procedures to be followed when programs appear "invulnerable" to change need to be measured against Warren's concern that such evaluative procedures may make an unintended contribution to that invulnerability.

Warren's concerns are stated as follows: the latent function of much impact evaluation research is that of reinforcing the major thrust of agency programs directing attention to problems of fine tuning of existing intervention strategies and away from causal patterns imbedded into the institutional structure. Thus, reinforcing a conception that agency service approaches are essentially on the "right track" and that the problem lies not with the larger institutional structure or even with the structure of the service system but primarily with how best to deal with aberrant individuals who are the real root of the problem and hence the appropriate target of intervention.

Warren observes further that the acceptance of agency problem definitions and the choice of research problems and methodologies in terms of the impact of fragmented intervention techniques on a target population, carry with them specific theoretical and ideological positions, usually unstated or even unexamined, which have an effect which is parallel to, and perhaps greater than, the effect of the reporting of the specific findings of the evaluation.

Warren's image of the "social scientist diagnostician" investigating critically, using the method of "informed rational analysis" and developing proposals for program alternatives is not reassuring on this point. To prescribe alternative interventive strategies requires, of course, moving beyond theory and data to value judgments.

A prescriptive posture must presume a "specific theoretical and ideological position" which Warren also leaves unstated and even unexamined much as he accuses the evaluation technician of doing. It is not reassuring to be presented with the image of a value-free social scientist capable of probing the etiology of social problems and presenting programs for action based upon fact, rather than upon institutional or other value biases. Such a position, as suggested by Martin Rein (1970), seems based upon the view that analysis of social problems, and the remedies proposed for reducing or eliminating them, are essentially technical rather than ideological and that science can somehow supercede moral and ideological speculation, a position I find no less alarming than the problem cited by Warren of the evaluator's unintended legitimation of the status quo.

Given these views of the human service system, and the

evaluator's role as an actor in that system, what methods are proposed?

Despite the obvious differences which the speakers have with each other, and, mine with parts of what each had to say, it is clear that substantial areas of agreement do exist and that the proposals made are parts of a total evaluation methodology. The differences are largely those of emphasis. I will not recapitulate all of the material on methodology but will focus on points of special interest to me.

Challenging prevailing definitions of the problem to be solved. I consider Warren's point on the importance of problem definition and its prescriptive implications for the articulation of program objectives, program strategies and service tactics critically important to evaluation research. Problems defined as due to the deficiencies of people having those problems can only lead to interventions designed to overcome those inadequacies. Nagi in his discussion of factors influencing gate-keeping decisions cites the tendencies of psychiatrists employing organically-based explanatory systems to employ organic treatment modalities, while the psychoanalytically oriented psychiatrist tends toward clinical approaches. Explanatory systems are clearly prescriptive. Significant modification of program objectives and program strategies and service tactics seem essentially impossible without continuous re-examination of the explanatory system used to define the problem under study. How we define the problem to be solved must ultimately determine what we do in problem-solving.

Warren's and Higgs' proposal that the evaluative process include an effort to gather what is known or has been hypothesized about the nature of the problem and about interventive strategies, seems to me especially well taken. I share the expressed admiration for Rivlin's work (1971). In that work she points out that the first step in making public policy is to get a picture of what the problem is: How many people are poor? Who are they? Where are they? Why are they poor? Such information can explode some myths and throw a good deal of light on policy choices. That fuller knowledge challenges prevailing problem definitions and is crucial to any effort at social action to change policies, strategies and tactics.

Information systems in the adversary process. Weiss sets out alternative evaluation models, namely (1) social experiments; (2) traditional evaluation; (3) accountability systems. If I understand his position, I would judge Higgs to be in substantial agreement with the value and appropriate use of these alternative methods. I would like to focus especially on Weiss's interest in the value of on-going information systems which can generate descriptive and evaluative information as well as data on the constraints that limit program performance and which can in turn provide useful guidance for decision making. According to Weiss, the key characteristic of an accounting system is to provide the information the different publics (funders, clients, organizations, etc.) have defined as relevant to their values and needs. A solid and reliable information system is certainly of critical importance to informed judgment. The observation by Weiss and others at this symposium suggests, however, the concurrent presence of different audiences, different publics with different values and different needs and most probably with different degrees of command over program resources, including information systems. It may be that the image of a single information system or evaluation procedure serving the values and needs of all such audiences concurrently, is unreal. Higgs, in what appears to be a confusing contradiction to his major thesis, suggests that evaluation serve no audience directly, that the evaluator have stakes independent of the client and subjects of the experiment. It is not immediately clear to me how evaluation as a process can be a tool primarily for action, scientific and inevitably political and how the evaluator as an actor in that process is to have no stake in the success of the experimental program being tested. An evaluation process which attempts to serve the interests of program managers, or, one which attempts to serve no specific interests, may not be as useful as an evaluation system conceived of as an adversary process in which different users of information become partisan advocates of their own interests using evaluation methods specific to their need for information to support them in achieving goals articulated on a basis other than research.

All human service programs serve multiple objectives as a consequence of the interplay of juxtaposed interests and conflicting constructions of reality which are so regularly aggregated in the legislative process. Coke and Hansan referred to this extensively in their comments. They noted that broad aim programs frequently have vague, often conflicting objectives as a consequence of a legislative process with many objectives, each with different constitutiencies, using different measuring sticks. In the process of administration, different objectives are weighted differently and change through time further complicating the problem of analysis. Different constituencies, for example, have differing levels of commitment to system maintenance, system control and system change objectives. This goal mix may be difficult or impossible to specify in a way acceptable to different constituent groups. The objective sought, or the rank-ordering of different objectives, will have everything to do with the evaluation outcome making very different results for the same program possible (i.e., public assistance). For the professional practitioner whose practice is directed to the achievement of goals not fully congruent with those of his employing agency, a total evaluation enterprise may include an adversary model in which he and his clients seek to develop an independent evaluation capability. Nagi in his discussion of "alternatives to validity" notes the increasing awareness of the vast imbalance in power when organizations are compared to individuals. This imbalance is even greater in regard to individuals in need of services and resources controlled by given organizations. Given the observations made in Nagi's paper, it may be that multiple modes of concurrent evaluation, of the same program, by different publics, is in order, including assurance of due process, the right of appeal, the ombudsman role, consumer advocate organizations. In this sense, evaluation is part of a political process, aided by rational methods of inquiry, and requiring multiple, concurrent, independently funded and administered programs reflecting the varieties of constituent needs and values which bear upon the problem.

No administrator, evaluator, or social scientist is, in my judgment, sufficiently competent to be the sole interpreter of other people's vital interests.

Duncan (See Chapter 5 Commentary) stresses the need for focus upon clients as (1) users of data; (2) decision-makers; (3) a special audience with their own goals and expectations for service. He advocates that evaluation be structured to include a client perspective.

That perspective seems to me unlikely in an evaluation

procedure which seeks consensus on the definition of goals and objectives. Alternative models have been suggested by the participants as follows:

1. An adversary system of evaluation which provides information needed by the client system for the effective pursuit of self-interest in the political system.
2. A market place system, as suggested by Weiss, based upon vouchers and cash payments and which offers multiple suppliers of needed services, allows client choice, stimulates agency accountability and responsiveness to client interests.

What is sought is the fuller exercise of the clients' right to vote in both the political and market systems.

Much more thought, it seems to me, needs to be given to the special conceptual and methodological problems confronted by consumer groups, professional organizations, citizens organizations wanting to develop an independent investigative capability able to generate data needed for the regular monitoring of service systems. Access to and the control over information can be central to the client's efforts to overcome a position of powerlessness in the organization, to participate in the process of policy formulation and program development and to increase the possibility that clients will not indiscriminately be denied services and benefits.

Program development. Warren's observations concerning multiple causation are especially apt. In most problem situations there is no single element which either causes the problem condition or can be used to correct or measurably ameliorate the problem condition. The result is that no single interventive technique can make a significant measurable impact upon such admittedly complex situations.

We need to think more broadly about service systems, programing more effectively to achieve broader-aim goals. Coke and Hansan have commented on the difficulties involved in evaluating broad-aim programs. Weiss and Rein (1969) point out that experimental design is poorly adapted to general aim programs, that is, to programs whose aims can be specified in many different ways. What is needed for evaluation of such programs is a more qualitative, process-oriented approach; an approach more descriptive and inductive; an approach concerned with describing the unfolding of the intervention reactions of individuals and institutions subjected to their impact; and approach that would lean toward the use of field methods emphasizing interviews and observation; an approach more concerned with learning than with measuring, and, with what happens than with whether it "works."

Given the present state of the art, the note of humility sounded by Weiss, and of the need for more experimental effort and learning, as sounded by all, seem very much in order.

I have learned a great deal from the review of these papers and the thought they inspire. A great deal has been omitted from this presentation. I am dependent upon your help in filling out and completing this summary and review of the major points made in these excellent papers.

REFERENCES

Rein, Martin, *Social Policy: Issues of Choice and Change.* New York: Random House, 1970.

Weiss, Robert S., and Martin Rein, "The Evaluation of Broad-Aim Programs: A Cautionary Case and A Moral." *The Annals*, Vol. 385, September 1969.

CHAPTER 10

A Bookshelf on Human Service
Program Evaluation

June G. Hopps
William C. Sze

Our society is increasingly one of planned social intervention. There is a plethora of human service programs dispersed administratively among many levels of government and private sector organizations. It is anticipated that they will have impact on the quality of life in America. There is also growing evidence that the paying public, the consuming public and the makers of public policy—groups that are not mutually exclusive—are not satisfied with the results of planned interventions for the improvement of social welfare. The public is likewise aware of the persistence of social ills and unmet needs despite allocations from both the public and private sectors to combat them. The experiences of the 1960's and particularly the War on Poverty has led to greater dialogue on the effectiveness of major social programs.

The purpose of this chapter is to provide an introduction to the general evaluation research literature. The domain and essential elements of evaluation research is defined and a general conceptual framework is provided to view the various evaluation research approaches. Finally, an extensive bookshelf is provided.

Domain of Evaluation Research

Evaluation research may be viewed as essentially an extension of the methodologies of "classical or basic research" in the social sciences. The classical research methodologies make use of the pre-post or experimental design method to assess the incidence and concentration patterns of social problems, their behavioral manifestations and the causal relations between problems or variables. The explicit antecedent of evaluation research may readily be seen in the "experimental design" variant of the classical research method. Here, the researcher intervened by the application of, or the withholding of, certain treatments to selected groups. In its simplest embodiment, the

The writers wish to thank Dr. Wyatt C. Jones, Professor of Research, The Florence Heller School for Advanced Studies in Social Welfare, Brandeis University, for reviewing this chapter.

"experimental design" consists of performing identical sets of measurements upon two different groups, an experimental group to which some prescribed treatment is given and the control group for which this treatment is either withheld or unavailable. Various techniques such as simple, stratified, cluster and combination sampling, are available to generate random samples which statistically insure the equality of the two groups prior to treatment. Evaluation research is identical in many aspects to its explicit antecedent, the experimental design. It also involves the active intervention of the experimenter administering treatment, which in the more general context of evaluation research may be a program or project of arbitrary scope. The techniques and analytical tools of evaluation research and classical experimental design are also virtually identical. By contrast however, classical experimentation has been correlational in the focus of its results. It should be noted that the concept of correlations is not entirely omitted in the overall process of evaluation research. In this instance, however, they are explicitly or implicitly "presumed" in the design of the intervention strategy rather than "tested for" in the research. Basic (classical) research, according to Cherns, arises out of the perceived needs of an academic discipline whereas action (evaluation) research is concerned with an (ongoing) problem in an organizational framework and involves the introduction and observation of planned change.[1] Other contrasts offered by Cherns relates to the generality and diffusivity of the research. He attributes to basic research great potential for generality but limited potential for immediate utilization whereas evaluative research is characterized by limited potential for generality but great potential for immediate utilization.[2] Suchman contrasts the concern of basic research with problems of theoretical significance to the concern of evaluation research with problems of administrative consequences.[3] In drawing contrast as Cherns and Suchman have done, one must, however, exercise caution. As Caro points out, basic research, even that not involving direct intervention on the part of the researcher, may be quite applicable to social action and have immediate administrative consequences.[4] According to present terminology such research may be said to be applicable within the general context of "evaluation" but would not constitute "evaluation research." Suchman has noted, in distinguishing evaluation from evalua-

ion research that: "*Evaluation* . . . the general social process
)f making judgments of worth regardless of the basis for such
udgments, and *evaluation research* . . . the use of the scientific
nethod for collecting data concerning the degree to which
;ome specified activity achieves some desired effect."[5] Carol
Weiss draws a similar distinction in her paper that is a part of
this volume.[6] Several other definitions of evaluation research
are to be found in the literature and there seems to be no
consensus definition. This is not surprising in view of the fact
that evaluation researchers have varying orientations, styles
and preferences. Yet, it is perhaps well to simply pinpoint the
key conceptual elements that are common to various definitions. These fundamental elements lead us to the inferences
that evaluation research is principally concerned with:

1) The effectiveness of the program in achieving its
desired goals, when such goals are explicit;
2) The impact of a program upon a target population,
especially when program objectives are not clearly
defined;
3) The manner in which a program achieves its goal or
makes its impact;
4) And efficiency, in terms of the expenditures of funds
and manpower versus the "presumed" desirability of
results, with which a program achieves its goal or
makes it impact.

In essence, evaluation research is an effort to determine and
delineate changes which take place in and as a result of
programs, or program components, by comparing results
(outputs) with stated program goals and identifying the degree
to which a program is responsible for these changes.[7]

Trends in Evaluation Research

Including the basic evaluation research models and all of
their variants, one finds that a large number of specific
methodologies have emerged in the course of their evolution
and development. Conceptually, it seems that the elements of
this collection of methodologies, or models, may be principally
distinguished according to whether their basic orientation is
skewed towards the outcome of social intervention, the process
of social intervention, or whether they seek to effect a balance
between outcome and process considerations. Within each
generic class of models one can also make distinctions based

upon the time-frame for execution of the evaluation research and thus for the availability of the management and decision-making information generated by the evaluation. The ensuing discussion treats the various evaluation research models within the conceptual frameworks that we have outlined. These models fall within the rubric of evaluation research and not evaluation, following the theme of this book. We have consistently noted that evaluation research involves an intervention whereas evaluation does not.

Outcome-Oriented Evaluation. In performing evaluation research one is often principally seeking to measure the final impact or effect, suitably defined, of a given intervention strategy upon a designated target population, giving less consideration to evaluation of the means by which the degree of the results is achieved. The "outcome-oriented" evaluation research model in this situation is frequently referred to as Impact Evaluation. From a methodological point of view impact evaluation is performed in much the same manner as the classical experimental design, the focus of its results being impactive rather than correlational. It is to be emphasized that the process or intervention strategy is of critical importance. Attention to it is given in the planning phases of the program. The choice of programs and strategies involve certain explicit or implicit assumptions or theories concerning the response of the target population to certain stimuli. These assumptions, carefully analyzed in the planning process, are, however, only indirectly tested in the impact evaluation approach. Further, the delivery process also goes untested in impact evaluation.

Management by Objectives represents another member of the "outcome-oriented" class of evaluation research models. Relative to impact evaluation, the orientation in this case is even further skewed towards concerns with outcome. This approach has been borrowed by the social sciences from the cadre of management tools of the business world where in some instances the methods of achieving the desired objectives have become, to within the limitations imposed by laws and some fairly flexible standards of business ethics, largely irrelevant. Such an extreme imbalance, however, would have quite serious ramifications in the social service sector. The paper by Nagi in this volume clearly elucidates some of the inherent pitfalls in the management by objectives approach to evaluation research.[8]

The availability of high speed, large capacity data process-ing hardware and systems has had a profound effect on "outcome-oriented" evaluation research, and as we shall later see, on the other classes of evaluation research. It has extended the capability and power of the basic tools of mathematical analysis and inference but more significant perhaps has been its effect upon the time frame during which relatively large scale evaluation research may be performed. At its inception, evaluation research was commenced at the end of a program or project. The collection of data was of course an ongoing process. With increased capacity to handle, process and analyze data we've seen the advent of "dynamic" or "on-line" variants of our basic "outcome-oriented" models. They gener-ally fall into two temporal classes, the discrete models and the continuous models. In the discrete models, program outcome information is available for management decision-making at one or more time points during the administering of the program. The natural extension of these discrete models are of course the continuous or at least quasi-continuous models. Examples of such continuous "outcome-oriented" evaluation research models would be Higgs' goal-oriented dynamic feedback technique[9] and Hoffer's PERT/Time System.[10] The use of such dynamic or on-line models in practical circumstances, however, may often be precluded by research resources availability, for example, computers, programmers and data processors.

Process-Oriented Evaluation. In distinction to the class of evaluation research models that focuses principally on out-come is the class of models where the focus of concern is weighted more heavily towards the process by which the social service is delivered or the proposed intervention effected. For conceptual purposes, evaluation research within the "process-oriented" class may be distinguished according to whether the evaluation is aimed at elements of the social service delivery system or rather, at the composite system itself. In the first instance the evaluation research takes on the character of the old "efficiency analysis" methodology of business and industry. Here, major attention is paid to program accounting and to the monitoring of client contacts and the performance of internal tasks. This involves the maintenance and subsequent analysis of fairly detailed records of individual and project activities. Such records, for example might supply quantitative data on the number of clients exposed to programs and the extent of the actual practitioner-client contacts. On the larger scale, "process-oriented" evaluation research takes on the character of "operations research" in which the social service delivery organization itself or some component thereof, is targeted by the evaluation, being treated as a composite system and with the evaluation directed toward assessing the overall consistency of organizational policy, task definition and resource allocation.

Problems associated with the political and organizational context in which evaluation research is performed are acutely manifested in "process-oriented" evaluation research. This intrinsic vulnerability is due to the very nature (as is commonly perceived) of this class of models: they, in effect, evaluate people and organizations as opposed to generally less personal entities such as programs or strategies. On the objective side, however, this class of evaluation research model can be invaluable in determining administrative viability and may provide a basis of screening programs (not necessarily people or organizations) on the basis of ability to establish contacts with clients and the cost of practitioner-client contacts.

The impact of computer technology has also been felt within this category of evaluation research. The dynamic variants of both the accountability-efficiency models and the operations research models are pronouncedly manifest in current "process-oriented" methodologies. In fact, the current usage of some of the terms themselves, e.g., operations research and accountability systems, have implicit dynamic connotations.

Balanced Outcome-Process Models. The underlying modality of this class of evaluation research models is their attempt to combine many of the most desirable features of the "outcome-oriented" class of models and the "process-oriented" class of models into a balanced system of analysis and decision-making. The most familiar members of this class of models are the "Cost-Benefit" analysis systems, the "Planning, Programming and Budgeting System" (PPBS), and the "Program Evaluation and Review Technique (PERT)".

The term cost-benefit explicitly indicates concern with the problems of outcome (benefit) and the problems of process (cost). Conceptually it is perhaps the simpler of the three systems mentioned. It is designed to answer questions about choices between alternative policies and programs available for achieving a specific social outcome or impact. In this sense it is a useful tool in best-use decision-making. The principal requirements of applying such a system is the ability to make assessments of costs and benefits. Generally in application to social service delivery one must consider costs which are both financial and non-financial in nature. An even more difficult problem, however is the assessment of benefits. Here, there is the inherent need to "quantify" these benefits, e.g., the number of consumer-program contacts, or some quantitative measure of the quality of that program-consumer contact. A major difficulty lies in the specification of goals; often they are either undefined or are unranked in priority. In such cases, the question of ability to quantify benefits becomes purely academic. Of course if program benefits can't be clearly specified, then neither can viable alternatives. It is not unusual to distinguish between cost-benefit analysis performed before and after a program of intervention. For example, Cain and Hollister use the terminology "a priori" and "ex post" cost-benefit analysis.[11] Technically, however, only the "ex post" analysis mode constitutes evaluation research, the "a priori" analysis mode falling within the more general framework of evaluation.

The PPBS, developed in the defense department under McNamara in 1965 and adopted by HEW in the following year, is an outgrowth of systems theory. Like the general systems approach it views the social service delivery organization and its programs as an interconnected complex of functionally related components or sub-systems. This model, because of its intended comprehensiveness, tends to be more complex than other evaluation research models. Two key contributing factors to this complexity is the inherent conflicts in sub-level or sub-system goals and the intrinsic parasitic nature of certain processes. To elaborate briefly, let us consider the organizational structure of the Welfare Department, State of Ohio. The Department is organized into three major sub-systems: policies and programs, service delivery, and management—plus the executive office. In effort to make service delivery the central thrust of the total system and to insure its optimal functioning, the goals and optimal functioning of the two other sub—systems often come into competition with the strong service delivery thrust. Additionally, some functions, like personnel recruitment and hiring, are dependent upon the three major sub-systems. In its most ideal form then, PPBS addresses the task of optimizing policies, programs and funds towards the achievement of primary goals under conditions in which sub-goals are at least partially conflicting, and in which efficiency or effectiveness of a decision in a given sub-system or component may be diminished by a second decision (equally good on an absolute basis) made in the same or a different sub-system or component.

It is worthwhile to compare the PPBS with Operations Research. In the sense that Operations Research aims at comprehensiveness, it is quite similar to PPBS, both models falling within the general systems theory framework. It is therefore not surprising to see these models treated as virtually identical.[12] In the present conceptualization, however, we draw a distinction between these two models which is based upon several important, though possibly subtle, aspects. The first is the more pronounced emphasis of PPBS on the outcome of program interventions and strategies and the associated implications for policy and planning. It gives more coarse-grained considerations to the operational problems as contrasted with the fine-grained analysis given by typical Operations Research. For example, one finds as typical applications of Operations Research the solution of such problems as inventory control, replacement and maintenance proce: ?s, production scheduling and waiting-time processes. Finally the PPBS has the characteristic of being more nearly integrated into the organization or program so that the evaluation research is apt to be more accepted in the planning and budgeting cycles.[13]

Evaluation Design Components

The models discussed above represent the current major approaches to evaluation research. When various approaches are compared, three basic components emerge either explicitly or implicitly and/or with differences in degree of emphasis as the critical elements required of any evaluative research model.

(1) Provision of outcome information. Emphasis is placed on information gathering and outcome data. Attempts are made to use methods that produce objective, systematic results in the measurement of the effort, effect, process and efficiency of program interventions. Numerous publications address this

issue including Edward Suchman,[14] B.G. Greenberg[15] and Michael Brooks.[16]

(2) Provision of information relating to the desirability of continuing or not continuing a program effort. Proponents and contributors to the idea of the social value judgment thrust in evaluation include Scriven and Glass. They assert that evaluative research must measure the performance of program data against a goal scale[17] and give an account of the worth and social utility of a program[18]

(3) Provision of clarity about the subject to be evaluated. It is indeed difficult to be clear about the subject of evaluation since the focus of interest on a given subject shifts dependent upon one's constituent group, i.e., administrator, researcher, client, consumer, and/or funder. Representatives of these pertinent groups are likely to view the goals of a program differently and likewise, expect different results. Inherent, therefore, is the prospect of conflicting views and opinions on outcomes. In achieving clarity, the delineation of focus becomes essential. The focus of a particular program could be in a number of areas. For example, it could be on "administrative efficiency." Here the issue and concerns could include problems on the worker-client ratio necessary for effective service delivery; the advantages of decentralized versus centralized programs; the trade-offs on the use of para-professionals as compared to an academically trained professional staff. Another example of the focus of evaluation research is related to outcome: "Do clients improve after receiving counseling?" Or the focus might be on "how well the services were given," or on the "process of change"—what happened, to whom did it happen and how did it happen?[19]

In addition to the need for clarity on "focus," there must be clarity on the "level" at which evaluation studies are conducted. Is the study to be focused on the "individual client," "a group of clients," the "individual project" (the neighborhood youth core center); "all youth programs" (all programs serving youth) in a given geographical area; or a combination of given "levels."

Evaluation at the Crossroads

The current state of the art of evaluation research in social services is composed of a large multiplicity of methodologies that have either evolved from the fundamental notions of classical research or that have been transferred with appropriate modification from business and industry and from the general theory of the behavior of multi-component systems. This multiplicity of evaluation research models reflect in part the amenability of certain types of intervention programs and social service delivery systems to particular kinds of evaluation research models. In spite of this apparently adequate collection of evaluation research methodologies, very little good evaluation research has been produced in the field of social services. It is incumbent upon today's evaluation researcher to understand clearly the basis for this situation and to devise plans for its elimination. The way that we deal with this problem will determine the course of evaluation research in the ensuing years.

Many of the problems associated with performing good evaluation research and which contribute to its lack of viability, have been discussed by the contributors to this volume. Evaluation research is beset at the very outset by the political and organizational context in which it must be performed. Even when these problems can be resolved, or more likely averted, there still remains fundamental technological problems of design, many of which are associated with the lack of adequate goal definition or weighting and the often inherent conflicts in some of these. Further there is no consensus on the optimum evaluation research model to be used for particular kinds of programs. These problems are "microscopic" in nature in that they are relevant to specific evaluation research efforts. It is clear that further viability of evaluation research dictates some retrenchment, directed towards the de-bugging and increased applicability of existing models.

A Bookshelf

The references included here are organized in the same manner as the general organization of this volume. Hence, the Macroscopic section consists of those references relating to Social, Political and Organizational aspects. The Technological section is organized by (1) presenting a list of general references which deals with methodological issues in general, and (2) separating human services into four major areas, namely, Social Service, Social Action Programs, Mental Health, and Health Care.

This "bookshelf" is not exhaustive as we recognize many

other worthwhile research reports and literature that cannot all be included in this chapter. We do feel, however, that the references included will give a solid foundation of knowledge in human service program evaluation.

The Macroscopic References

Adams, R.N. and J.J. Preiss (eds.), *Human Organization Research: Field Relations and Techniques.* Homewood, Illinois: Dorsey. 1960.

Bator, Francis M., *The Question of Government Spending: Public Needs and Private Wants.* New York: Harper & Row. 1960.

Blau, Peter M. and W.R. Scott, *Formal Organizations: A Comparative Approach.* San Francisco: Chandler. 1962.

Chase, Samuel B. Jr., (ed.), *Problems in Public Expenditure Analysis.* Washington, D.C.: Brookings Institution. 1968.

DeBie, Pierre, "Problem-focused Research." *Main Trends of Research in the Social and Human Sciences.* Chapter 9. UNESCO. Place de Fontenoy, Paris. 1970. pp. 578-644.

Darfman, Robert (ed.), *Measuring Benefits of Government Investments.* Washington D.C.: Brookings Institution. 1965.

Etzioni, Amitai and Edward W. Lehman, "Some Dangers in Valid Social Measurement." *The Annals.* September 1967. pp. 1-15.

Fairweather, George, *Methods of Experimental Social Innovation.* New York: John Wiley & Sons, Inc. 1967.

Fanshel, David (ed.), *Research in Social Welfare Administration: Its Contributions and Problems.* New York: National Association of Social Workers. 1962.

Freeman, Howard E. and Clarance C. Sherwood, *Social Research and Social Policy.* Englewood Cliffs, New Jersey: Prentice-Hall, 1970.

Gore, William J., *Administrative Decision-Making: A Heuristic Model.* New York: John Wiley & Sons, Inc. 1964.

Gross, Bertram M., *State of the Nation: Social System Accounting.* London: Associate Book Publishers. 1966.

——————————, *The Managing of Organizations.* New York: Free Press. 1964.

Harris, C.W., *Problems in Measuring Change.* Madison: University of Wisconsin Press. 1963.

Harris, Joseph P., *Congressional Control of Administration.* Washington, D.C.: The Brookings Institution. 1964.

Hovey, Harold A., *The Planning, Programming, Budgeting Approach to Government Decision Making.* New York: Frederick A. Praeger. 1968.

Jones, Roger W., "The Model as a Decision-Maker's Dilemma."*Public Administration Review.* Vol. 24. 1964. pp. 158-160.

Kaplan, Abraham, *The Conduct of Inquiry.* San Francisco: Chandler Publishing Co. 1964.

Mann, John, "Technical and Social Difficulties in the Conduct of Evaluative Research."*Changing Human Behavior.* New York: Scribners. 1965.

Merton, Robert K. and Robert A. Nisbet (eds.), *Contemporary Social Problems.* New York: Harcourt, Brace & World Co. 1966.

Mullen, Edward J. and James R. Dumpson (eds.), *Evaluation of Social Intervention.* San Francisco: Jossey-Bass, Inc. 1972.

Myrdal, Gunnar, *Objectivity in Social Research.* New York: Pantheon Books. 1969.

Nagi, Saad and Roland Corwin (eds.), *The Social Contexts of Research.* New York: John Wiley & Sons, 1972.

Penick, James L., Jr., *et al.* (eds.), *The Politics of American Science: 1939 to the Present.* Chicago: Rand Mc Nally. 1965.

Rivlin, Alice M., *Systematic Thinking for Social Action.* Washington, D.C.: The Brookings Institution. 1971.

Russett, Bruce M., *et al., World Handbook of Political and Social Indicators.* New Haven, Connecticut: Yale University Press. 1964.

Shubik, Martin, "Studies and Theories of Decision Making." *Administrative Science Quarterly.* Vol. 3. 1958. pp. 290-399.

Sjoberg, Gideon (ed.), *Ethics, Politics and Social Research.* Cambridge, Massachusetts: Schenkman Publishing Co. 1967.

Sonneborn, T.M. (ed.), *The Control of Human Heredity and Evolution.* New York: Macmillan, 1965.

Weiss, Carol H., "The Politicization of Evaluation Research." *Journal of Social Issues.* Vol. 26. No. 4. 1970. pp. 57-68.

Westin, Alan F. (ed.), *Information Technology in a Democracy.* Cambridge: Harvard University Press. 1970.

Williams, W. and J. Evans, "The Politics of Evaluation: The Case of Headstart." *Annals.* Vol. 385. September 1969. pp. 118-132.

————————, *Social Policy Research and Analysis.* New York: American Elsevier. 1971.

Wolin, Sheldon S., *Politics and Vision.* Boston: Little Brown. 1960.

Zald, Mayer N. (ed.), *Power in Organization.* Nashville, Tennessee: Vanderbilt University Press. 1970.

The Technological References

General References

Ackoff, Russell L., "The Development of Operations Research as a Science." *Operations Research.* Vol. 4. June 1956. pp. 265-295.

Bateman, Worth, "Assessing Programs' Effectiveness," *Welfare in Review.* Vol. 6. January/February 1968. pp. 1-10.

Campbell, Donald T., "Factors Relevant to the Validity of Experiments in Social Settings." *Psychological Bulletin.* Vol. 54, 1957. pp. 297-311.

————————, and Julian Stanley, *Experimental and Quasi-Experimental Design for Research.* Chicago: Rand-McNally. 1963.

Caro, Francis G. (ed.), *Readings in Evaluation Research.* New York: Russell Sage Foundation. 1971.

Carter, Genevieve W., "The Challenge of Accountability— How We Measure the Outcomes of Our Efforts." *Public Welfare.* Summer, 1971. pp. 267-277.

Eaton, Joseph W., "A Scientific Basis for Helping," in Alfred J. Kahn, *Issues in American Social Work.* New York: Columbia University Press. 1965. pp. 270-292.

————————, "Symbolic and Substantive Evaluation

Research." *Administrative Science Quarterly.* Vol. 6. No. 4. 1962. pp. 421-442.

Glock, Charles Y. (ed.), *Survey Research in the Social Sciences.* New York: Russell Sage Foundation. 1967.

Helmer, Olaf, *Social Technology.* New York: Basic Books. 1966.

Herzog, Elizabeth, "Research Demonstrations and Common Sense." *Child Welfare.* June 1962. pp. 243-247.

——————————, *Some Guidelines for Evaluative Research.* Washington: U.S. Department of Health, Education and Welfare, Social Security Administration. Children's Bureau Publication 375. 1959.

Hesseling, P., "Principles of Evaluation." *Social Compass.* Vol. 11. No. 1. 1964. pp. 5-22.

Hillier, Frederick S. and Gerald J. Lieberman, *Introduction to Operations Research.* San Francisco: Holden-Day, Inc. 1967.

Hinrichs, Harley H. and Graeme M. Taylor, *Program Budgeting and Benefit-Cost Analysis: Cases, Text and Readings.* Pacific Palisades, California: Goodyear Publishing Co. 1969.

Hyman, H.H., T.W. Hopkins and Charles Wright, *Application of Methods of Evaluation.* Berkeley: University of California Press. 1962.

Jenkins, John G., "Validity for What?" *Journal of Consulting Psychology.* Vol. 10. 1946. pp. 93-98.

Klineberg, Otto, "The Problem of Evaluation Research." *International Social Science Bulletin.* Vol. 7. No. 3. 1955.

Lyden, Fremont J. and Ernest G. Miller (eds.), *Planning, Programing, Budgeting: A Systems Approach to Management.* Chicago: Markham Publishing Co. 1968.

Morse, Philip M. (ed.), *Operations Research for Public Systems.* Cambridge: Massachusetts Institute of Technology Press. 1967.

Oslon, Mancur, *Social Indicators and Social Accounts.* Washington, D.C.: U.S. Government Printing Office. 1968.

O'Toole, Richard (ed.), *The Organization, Management and Tactics of Social Research.* Cambridge, Massachusetts: Schenkman Publishing Co. 1971.

Polansky, Norman A. (ed.), *Social Work Research*. The University of Chicago Press. 1960.

Rivett, Patrick, *An Introduction to Operations Research*. New York: Basic Books. 1968.

Rossi, Peter H. and Walter Williams (eds.), *Evaluating Social Programs*. New York: Seminar Press. 1972.

Sheldon, Eleanor B. and Wilbert E. Moore (eds.), *Indicators of Social Change: Concepts and Measurements*. New York: Russell Sage Foundation. 1968.

Tripodi, Tony, Phillip Fellin and Irwin Epstein, *Social Program Evaluation*. Itasca, Illinois: F.E. Peacock Publishers, Inc. 1971.

Twain, David, Eleanor Harlow and Donald Merwin, *Research and Human Services*. New York: Research and Development Center. Jewish Board of Guardians. 1970.

U.S. Department of Health, Education, and Welfare, *Toward a Social Report*. Washington, D.C.: U.S. Government Printing Office. 1969.

Warren, Roland, *Social Research Consultation*. New York: Russell Sage Foundation. 1963.

Webb, Eugene, *Unobtrusive Measures: Nonreactive Research in the Social Sciences*. Chicago: Rand McNally and Co. 1966.

Weiss, Carol H., *Evaluation Research: Methods for Assessing Program Effectiveness*. Englewood Cliffs, New Jersey: Prentice-Hall, Inc. 1972.

_____, *Evaluating Action Programs: Readings in Social Action and Education*. Boston: Allyn & Bacon, Inc. 1972.

Weiss, Robert C. and Martin Rein, "The Evaluation of Broad-Aim Programs: A Cautionary Case and a Moral." *Annals*. Vol. 385. September 1969. pp. 133-142.

Wholey, J., *Federal Evaluation Practices*. Washington, D.C.: The Urban Institute. 1969.

_____, *Program Evaluation in the Department of Health, Education and Welfare. Federal Program Evaluation Practices*. Washington, D.C.: The Urban Institute.

Social Service References

Aronson, Sidney H. and Clarence C. Sherwood, "Researcher Versus Practitioner: Problems in Social Action Research." *Social Work.* Vol. 12. No. 4. October 1967. pp. 89-96.

✗ Ballard, R. G. and Emily H. Mudd, "Some Sources of Difference Between Client and Agency Evaluation of Effectiveness of Counseling." *Social Casework.* Vol. 39. 1958. pp. 30-35.

Brown, G. E. (ed.), *The Multi-Problem Dilemma: A Social Research Demonstration with Multi-Problem Families.* Metuchen, N. J.: The Scarecrow Press, Inc. 1968.

Carter, Genevieve W., *The Social Indicators Movement: Perspective for Evaluation.* Monograph by Regional Research Institute in Social Welfare. Los Angeles, California: University of Southern California School of Social Work. March 1972.

———, *Research in Public Welfare: A Five-Year Review.* Monograph by Regional Research Institute in Social Welfare. Los Angeles, California: University of Southern California School of Social Work. December 1970.

Deutsch, M. and M. E. Collins, *Interracial Housing: A Psychological Evaluation of a Social Experiment.* Minneapolis: University of Minnesota Press. 1951.

✗ Elkin, Robert, "Analyzing Time, Costs, and Operations in a Voluntary Children's Institution and Agency." *Project on Cost Analysis in Children's Institutions.* Washington, D. C.: U. S. Department of Health, Education and Welfare. September 1965.

Ferman, Louis A., "Some Perspectives on Evaluating Social Welfare Programs." *Annals.* Vol. 385. September 1969. pp. 143-156.

Finestone, Samuel, "Some Requirements for Agency-Based Research," *Social Casework.* Vol. 44. March 1963. pp. 132-136.

Freeman, Howard E., "The Strategy of Social Policy Research," in *The Social Welfare Forum.* New York: Columbia University Press. 1963. pp. 142-156.

———, and H. A. Weeks, "Analysis of a Program of Treatment of Delinquent Boys." *American Journal of Sociology.* Vol. 62 1956. pp. 56-62.

Hunt, McViker and Leonard S. Kogan, *Measuring Results in Social Casework.* New York: Family Service Association of America. 1950.

Kitano, Harry H. L., "The Concept of 'Precipitant' in Evaluative Research." *Social Work.* Vol. 8. No. 4. October 1963. pp. 34-38.

Kogan, Leonard S., J. McVicker Hunt, and Phyliss F. Bartelme, *A Follow-up Study of the Results of Social Casework.* New York: Family Service Association of America. 1953.

Lehrman, Louis J., *et al, Success and Failure of Treatment in Child Guidance Clinics of the Jewish Board of Guardians, New York City.* New York: Jewish Board of Guardians. 1949.

Lerman, Paul, "Evaluative Studies of Institutions for Delinquents: Implications for Research and Social Policy." *Social Work.* Vol. 13. No. 3. July 1968. pp. 55-64.

Levine, Abraham S., "Cost-Benefit Analysis and Social Welfare Program Evaluation." *Social Service Review.* Vol. 42. June 1968. pp. 173-183.

Levinson, Perry. "Evaluation of Social Welfare Programs: Two Research Models." *Welfare in Review.* Vol. 4. 1966. pp. 5-12.

Mass, Henry S. (ed.), *Five Fields of Social Service: A Review of Research.* New York: National Association of Social Workers. 1966.

Meyer, Henry J., E. F. Borgatta, and W. C. Jones, *Girls at Vocational High: An Experiment in Social Work Intervention.* New York: Russell Sage Foundation. 1965.

Miller, S. M., "The Study of Man: Evaluating Action Programs."*Trans-Action.* Vol. 2. March/April 1965. pp. 38-39.

Mullen, Edward F. and James R. Dumpson (eds.), *Evaluation of Social Intervention.* San Francisco: Jossey-Bass, Inc. 1972.

Powers, Edwin and Helen Witmer, *An Experiment in the Prevention of Delinquency: Cambridge-Somerville Youth Study.* New York: Columbia University Press. 1951.

Schorr, Alvin, *Slums and Social Security: An Appraisal of the Effectiveness of Housing Policies in Helping to Eliminate Poverty in the United States.* Washington, D. C.: U. S. Social Security Administration. The Government Printing Office. 1963.

Schwartz, Edward G. and Martin Wolins, *Cost Analysis in Child Welfare.* Washington, D. C.: U. S. Department of

Health, Education and Welfare. Social Security Administration. Children's Bureau. Publication No. 366. 1958.

✗ Segal, Steven P., "Research on the Outcome of Social Work Therapeutic Interventions: A Review of the Literature." *Journal of Health and Social Behavior*. Vol. 13. No. 1. March 1972. pp. 3-17.

Stein, H. B., "The Study of Organizational Effectiveness," in *Research in Social Welfare Administration*, David Fanshel (ed.) New York: National Association of Social Workers. 1962. pp. 22-32.

————, George M. Hougham, and Serapio R. Zalba, "Assessing Social Agency Effectiveness: A Goal Model." *Welfare in Review*. Vol. 6. No. 2. 1968. pp. 13–18.

Thomas, Edward J., "A Research Evaluation of In-Service Training and of Reduced Workloads in Aid to Dependent Children, A Report of an Experiment Conducted in Michigan." *Public Welfare*. Vol. 16. 1958. pp. 109–132.

Vinter, Robert D., "Analysis of Treatment Organizations." *Social Work*. Vol. 8. No. 4. July 1963. pp. 3-15.

Witmer, Helen L. and E. Tufts, *The Effectiveness of Delinquency Prevention Programs*. Washington, D. C.: Children's Bureau, Publication No. 340. 1954.

Community Action Program References

Brooks, Michael P., "The Community Action Program as a Setting for Applied Research." *Journal of Social Issues*. Vol. 21. 1965. pp. 29-40.

Clark, Kenneth B., and Jeanette Hopkins, *A Relevant War Against Poverty: A Study of Community Action Programs and Observable Social Change*. New York: Harper and Row. 1968.

Clark, Terry N. (ed.), *Community Structure and Decision-Making: Comparative Analyses*. san Francisco: Chandler. 1968.

Elinson, J., "Effectiveness of Social Action Programs in Health and Welfare," in *Assessing the Effectiveness of Health Services Ross Conference on Pediatric Research*. Columbus, Ohio: Ross Laboratories. 1967. pp. 77-81.

Evans, John W., "Evaluating Social Action Programs," *Social Science Quarterly*. Vol. 50. No. 3, 1969. pp. 568-581.

Freeman, Howard E. and Clarence C. Sherwood. "Research

in Large-scale Intervention Programs." *Journal of Social Issues.* Vol. 21. No. 1. January 1965. pp. 11-28.

Hyman, Herbert H. and Charles R. Wright, "Evaluating Social Action Programs," in P. F. Lazarsfeld, W. N. Sewell, and H. L. Wilensky (eds.), *The Use of Sociology.* New York: Basic Books. 1967.

Kramer, Ralph M., *Participation of the Poor: Comparative Community Case Studies in the War on Poverty.* Englewood Cliffs, N. J.: Prentice-Hill. 1969.

Marris, Peter P. and M. Rein, *Dilemmas of Social Reform.* New York: Atherton Press. 1967.

Parsell, Alfred P., Dynamic Evaluation: The Systems Approach to Action Research. Santa Monica: Systems Development Corporation. 1966.

Rossi, Peter H., "Boobytraps and Pitfalls in the Evaluation of Social Action Programs."*Proceedings of the American Statistical Association.* Social Statistics Section, 1966.

_____"Evaluating Social Action Programs," *Trans-Action.* Vol. 4. No. 7. June 1967. pp. 51-53.

_____"Practice, Method, and Theory in Evaluating Social Action Programs, in James L. Sundquist (ed,), *On Fighting Poverty.* New York: Basic Books. 1969. pp. 217-234.

Sadofsky, Stanley, "Utilization of Evaluation Results: Feedback into the Action Program," in June L. Shmelzer, *Learning in Action.* Washington: Government Printing Office. 1966.

Sherwood, Clarence C., "Issues in Measuring Results of Action Programs." *Welfare in Review.* Vol. 5. No. 7. 1967. pp. 13-18.

Somers, Gerald G. and Ernst W. Stromsdorfer, "Neighborhood Youth Corps: A Nationwide Analysis." *The Journal of Human Resources.* Vol. 7. No. 4. Fall 1972. pp. 446-459.

Suchman, Edward A., *Evaluative Research: Principles and Practice in Public Service and Social Action Programs.* New York: Russell Sage Foundation. 1967.

Tripodi, Tony, Irwin Epstein and Carol MacMurray, "Dilemmas in Evaluation: Implications for Administrators of Social Action Programs." *American Journal of Orthopsychiatry.* Vol. 40. No. 5. October 1970. pp. 850-857.

Mental Health References

Bahn, A. K., "The Development of an Effective Statistical System in Mental Illness." *American Journal of Psychiatry.* Vol. 116. No. 9. March 1960. pp. 798-800.

Ballard, Robert G. and Emily H. Mudd, "Some Theoretical and Practical Problems in Evaluating Effectiveness of Counseling." *Social Casework.* Vol. 38. December 1957. pp. 533-538.

Beard, J. H., R. B. Pitt, S. H. Fisher and V. Goertzel, "Evaluating the Effectiveness of a Psychiatric Rehabilitation Program." *American Journal of Orthopsychiatry.* Vol. 33. No. 4. 1963. pp. 701-712.

Bellak, Leopold and Harvey Barten (eds.), *Progress in Community Mental Health.* New York: Grune and Stratton. 1969.

Blenkner, M., "Obstacles to Evaluative Research in Casework." *Social Casework.* Vol. 31, March 1950. pp. 97-105.

Brigante, Thomas R., "The Assessment Process in Campus Community Mental Health Programs." *Community Mental Health Journal.* Vol. 5. No. 2. April 1969. pp. 140-148.

Chassen, J. B., "Population and Sample: A Major Problem in Psychiatric Research." *American Journal of Orthopsychiatry.* Vol. 40. No. 3. April 1970. pp. 456-462.

⚹ Doab, Christopher B., "An Evaluation of 400 Mental Patients: Implications for Continuity and Change." *Journal of Health and Social Behavior.* Vol. 10. No. 3. September 1969. pp. 218-224.

Edwards, Allen L. and Lee J. Cronback, "Experimental Design for Research in Psychotherapy." *Journal of clinical Psychology.* Vol. 8. January 1952. pp. 51-59.

Eysenck, J. J., "The Effects of Psychotherapy: An Evaluation." *Journal of Consulting Psychology.* Vol. 16. 1952 pp. 319–324.

⚹ Freed, Harvey M., "Promoting Accountability in Mental Health Services." *American Journal of Orthopsychiatry.* Vol 42. No. 5. October 1972. pp. 761-770.

Freeman, Howard E. and Ozzie G. Simmons, "The Use of the Survey in Mental Illness Research." *Mental Hygiene.* Vol. 44. July 1960. pp. 400-410.

Garmezy, Norman, "Vulnerability Research and the Issue of Primary Prevention." *American Journal of Orthopsychiatry.* Vol. 41. No. 1. January 1971. pp. 149-157.

Glidwell, J. C., "Methods for Community Mental Health Research." *American Journal of Orthopsychiatry.* Vol. 27. January 1957. pp. 38-54.

Gruenberg, Ernest (ed.), "Evaluating the Effectiveness of Mental Health Services." *Milbank Memorial Fund Quarterly.* Vol. 44. Part 2. January 1966.

Guy, William and Gertrude M. Gross, "Problems in the Evaluation of Day Hospitals." *Community Mental Health Journal.* Vol. 3. No. 2. Summer 1967. pp. 111-118.

Harmon, Charles E. and Kenneth Meinhardt, "A Computer System for Treatment Evaluation at the Community Mental Health Center." *American Journal of Public Health.* Vol. 62. No. 12. December 1972. pp. 1596-1601.

Howe, Louisa P. "Problems in the Evaluation of Mental Health Programs," in Kotinsky, Ruth and Helen L. Witmer, *Community Programs for Mental Health.* Cambridge, Massachusetts: Harvard University Press. 1955. pp. 225-295.

Hutcheson, Bellenden R. and Elliott A. Krause, "Systems Analysis and Mental Health Services." *Community Mental Health Journal.* Vol. 5. No. 1. February 1969. pp. 29-45.

Jahoda, Marie, *Evaluation in Mental Health.* Washington, D. C.: U. S. Department of Health, Education, and Welfare. 1955.

Kiersuk, Thomas J. and Robert E. Sherman, "Goal Attainment Scaling: A General Method for Evaluating Comprehensive Community Mental Health Programs." *Community Mental Health Journal.* Vol. 4. No. 6. December 1968. pp. 443-453.

Kramer, Morton, *et al,* "National Approach to the Evaluation of Community Mental Health Programs." *American Journal of Public Health.* Vol. 51. No. 7. July 1961. pp. 969-979.

Lemkau, Paul V. and Benjamin Pasamanick, "Problems in Evaluation of Mental Health Programs." *American Journal of Orthopsychiatry.* Vol. 27. No. 1. 1957. pp. 55-58.

Levine, Rachel A., "Consumer Participation in Planning and Evaluation of Mental Health Services." *Social Work.* Vol. 15. No. 2. April 1970. pp. 41-46.

Levy, Leo, Allen N. Herzog and Elizabeth J. Slotkin, "The Evaluation of Statewide Mental Health Programs: A Systems Approach." *Community Mental Health Journal.* Vol. 4. No. 4. August 1968. pp. 340-349.

MacMahon, Brian, Thomas F. Pugh and George B Hutchison, "Principles in the Evaluation of Community Mental Health Programs." *American Journal of Public Health.* Vol. 51. July 1961. pp. 963-968.

Massarik, Fred A., *Sensitivity Training Impact Model: SOME First (and Second) Thoughts on the Evaluation of Sensitivity Training.* Washington, D. C.: National Training Laboratories. 1965.

May, Philip R. A., "Cost-efficiency of Mental Health Delivery Systems." *American Journal of Public Health.* Vol. 60. No. 11. November 1970. pp. 2060-2067.

Meyer, Henry J. and Edgar F. Borgatta, *An Experiment in Mental Patient Rehabilitation.* New York: Russell Sage Foundation. 1959.

Meyer, H. J. and E. F. Borgatta, "Paradoxes in Evaluating Mental Health Programs." *International Journal of Social Psychiatry.* Vol. 5. 1959. pp. 136-145.

Milbank Memorial Fund, *Planning Evaluation of Mental Health Programs.* New York. 1958.

Riedel, D., *et al,* "Psychiatric Utilization Review as Patient Care Evaluation." *American Journal of Public Health.* Vol. 62. No. 9. September 1972. pp. 1222-1228.

Roberts, Leigh M., Norman S. Greenfield, and Milton H. Miller (eds.), *Comprehensive Mental Health: The Challenge of Evaluation.* Madison, Wisconsin: The University of Wisconsin Press. 1968.

⁕ Schiff, Sheldon K., "Community Accountability and Mental Health Services." *Mental Hygiene.* Vol. 54. No. 2. April 1970. pp. 205-214.

Smith, William G. and Norris Hansell, "Territorial Evaluation of Mental Health." *Community Mental Health Journal.* Vol. 3. No. 2. Summer 1967. pp. 119-124.

Srole, Leo. *et al,* *Mental Health in the Metropolis.* New York: McGraw-Hill. 1962.

Stanton, A. H. and M. S. Schwartz, *The Mental Hospital: A Study of Instututional Participation in Psychiatric Illness and Treatment.* New York: Basic Books. 1954.

U. S. Department of Health, Education and Welfare. *Evaluation in Mental Health: A Review of the Problem of Evaluating Mental Health Activities.* Public Health Service, National Institute of Health, National Institute of Mental Health. Publication No. 413. 1955.

Wachs, Melvin W., "Planning-Programing-Budgeting and Management Information Systems for Mental Health." *American Journal of Public Health.* Vol. 59. No. 2. February 1969. pp. 261-266.

Wallace, Rains S., "Criteria for What? *American Psychologist.* Vol. 2. June 1965. pp. 416-425.

Wellner, Alfred M., Lewis M. Garmize, and Gregory Helweg, "Program Evaluation: A Proposed Model for Mental Health Services." *Mental Hygiene.* Vol. 54. No. 4. October 1970. pp. 530-534.

Whittington, H. G. and Charles Steenbarger, "Preliminary Evaluation of a Decentralized Community Mental Health Clinic." *American Journal of Public Health.* Vol. 60. No. 1. January 1970. pp. 64-77.

Yudin, Lee W. and Stephen I. Ring, "The Impact on Research and Evaluation." *American Journal of Orthopsychiatry.* Vol. 41. No. 1. January 1971. pp. 149-157.

Health Care References

Borgatta, Edgar F., "Research Problems in Evaluation of Health Service Demonstrations." *Milbank Memorial Fund Quarterly* Vol. 44. Part 2. October 1966.

Chein, Isadore, *et al, The Road to H.* New York: Basic Books. 1964.

Deniston, O. L. and I. M. Rosenstock, "Evaluating Health Programs." *Public Health Reports.* Vol. 85. No. 9. 1970. pp. 835-840.

Deniston, O. L., I. M. Rosenstock, W. Welch, and V. A. Getting, "Evaluation of Program Efficiency." *Public Health Reports.* Vol. 83. No. 7. 1968. pp. 603-610.

Donabedian, Avedis, "Evaluating the Quality of Medical Care." *Milbank Memorial Fund Quarterly.* Vol. 44. No. 3. Part 2. 1966. pp. 166-203.

Drew, Elizabeth R., "HEW Grapples with PPBS." *Public Interest.* Summer 1967. pp. 9-29.

Feldstein, Martin S., *Economic Analysis for Health Service Efficiency.* Chicago: Markham. 1968.

Getting, V. A., "Evaluation." *American Journal of Public Health.* Vol. 47. April 1957. pp. 408-413.

Greenberg, Bernard G. and Berwyn F. Mattison, "The Ways and Wherefores of Program Evaluation." *Canadian Journal of Public Health.* Vol. 46. July 1955. pp. 293-299.

Hawley, Paul R., "Evaluation of the Quality of Patient Care." *American Journal of Public Health.* Vol. 45. Dec. 1955. pp. 1533-1537.

Hilleboe, Herman E., "Improving Performance in Public Health." *Public Health Reports.* January 1964.

Hutchison, George B., "Evaluation of Preventive Services." *Journal of Chronic Diseases.* Vol. 11. May 1960. pp. 497-508.

James, George, "Research by Local Health Departments— Problems, Methods, Results." *American Journal of Public Health.* Vol. 48, March 1958. pp. 353-361.

Knutson, Andie L., "Evaluating Program Progress." *Public Health Reports.* Vol. 70. March 1955. pp. 305-310.

_____"Influence of Values on Evaluation." *Health Education Monograph.* Vol. 3. 1958. pp. 25-31.

McKeown, Thomas, *Medicine in Modern Society: Medical Planning Based on Evaluation of Medical Achievement.* New York: Hafner. 1966.

Osterweil, Jerry, "Evaluation: A Keystone of Comprehensive Health Planning." *Community Mental Health Journal.* Vol. 5. No. 2. April 1969. pp. 121-128.

Schonfeld, H. K., *et al,* "The Development of Standards for the Audit and Planning of Medical Care." *American Journal of Public Health.* Vol. 88. No. 11. November 1968. pp. 2097-2110.

Schulberg, Herbert C., Alan Cheldon, and Frank Baker(eds.), *Program Evaluation in the Health Fields.* New York: Behavioral Publications, Inc. 1969

Schulberg, Herbert C. and Frank Baker, "Program Evaluation Models and the Implementation of ResearchFindings." *American Journal of Public Health.* Vol. 58. No. 7. July 1968. pp. 1248-1255.

Simmons, W. R. and E. E. Bryant, "An Evaluation of Hospitalization Data From the Health Interview Survey." *American Journal of Public Health.* Vol. 52. October 1962. pp. 638-647.

Smith, W. F., "Cost-Effectiveness and Cost-Benefit Analyses for Public Health Programs." *Public Health Reports.* Vol. 83. No. 11. November 1968. pp. 899-906.

Solon, J. A., *et al,* "Patterns of Medical Care: Validity of Interview Information on Use of Hospital Clinics." *Journal of Health and Human Behavior.* Vol. 3. Spring 1962. pp. 21-29.

Suchman, Edward A., "Preventive Health Behavior: A Model for Research on Community Health Campaigns." *Journal of Health and Social Behavior.* Vol. 8. No. 3. September 1967. pp. 197–208.

Vickers, Geoffrey, "What Sets the Goals of Public Health?" *The Lancet.* Vol. 1. March 1958. pp. 599–602.

Footnotes for Chapter 10

[1] Albert Cherns, "Social Research and Its Diffusion." *Human Relations.* No. 22, (1969), pp. 209-218.

[2] *Ibid.*

[3] Edward Suchman, "Evaluating Educational Programs." *The Urban Review,* Vol. 3, No. 4, (February 1969), pp. 15-17.

[4] Frank Caro, "Evaluation Research: An Overview." *Readings in Evaluation Research,* (New York: Russel Sage Foundation, 1971), pp. 1-34.

[5] Edward Suchman, *op.cit.*

[6] Carol Weiss, "Alternative Models of Evaluation," in Chapter 5 of this volume.

[7] Abraham Levine, "Principles of Research Evaluation." *Social Service Delivery, Evaluation and Demonstration,* Conference proceedings: Regional Research Institute in Social Welfare, University of Southern California, 1970.

[8] Saad Z. Nagi, "When Norms of Validity Fail to Guide Gate-Keeping Decisions in Service Organizations," in Chapter 3 of this volume.

[9] Louis Higgs, "Experimental Design in Social Intervention Programs: Some Perspectives on Evaluation." in Chapter 4 of this volume.

[10] Joe R. Hoffer, "PERT: A Tool for Managing of Human Service Programs." *Planning for the Aging: Service Development and Coordination Through Area Agencies.* ed. Armand Louffer, (Ann Arbor, Michigan: Institute of Gerontology, 1973), Chapter 13.

[11] Glen G. Cain and Robinson G. Hallister, "The Methodology of Evaluating Social Action Programs," in *Evaluating Social Programs: Theory, Practice and Politics,* ed. Peter Rossi and Walter Williams. (New York: Seminar Press, 1972), pp. 109-137

[12] More see: Genevieve W. Carter, "The Challenge of Accountability— How we Measure the Outcomes of Our Efforts," *Public Welfare as Human Service* (Summer 1971) pp. 267-277.

[13] For a good discussion on Operrations Research, see C. West Churchman, Russel L. AAckoff and E. Leonard Arnoff, *Introduction to Operations Research* (New York: John Wiley & Sons, Inc.), 1957.

For PPBS, see: Arthur Spindler, "PPBS and Social Rehabilitation Services" *Welfare in review* (March-April, 1969), pp. 22-28.

[14] Edward Suchman, *Evaluation Research* (New York: Russell Sage Foundation, 1967).

[15] B. G. Greenberg, "Evaluation of Social Programs," *Review of the International Statistical Institute.* no. 36, pp. 260-277.

[16] Michael Brooks, "The Community Action Program as a Setting for Applied Research, *Journal of Social Issues*, no. 21, (1965), pp. 29-40.

[17] Michael Scriven,"The Methodology of Evaluation," in *Perspectives of Curriculum Evaluation* (Chicago: Rand McNally, 1967), pp. 39-83.

[18] Gene Glass, "The Growth of Evaluation Methodology," *AERA Curriculum Evaluation Monograph Series*, no. 7 (Chicago: Rand McNally, 1971).

[19] Helen Nothern, "Report of Work Groups," *Social Service Delivery, Education and Demonstration*, Conference Proceedings, Regional Research Institute, University of Southern California, 1970, pp. 35-38